ENGLAND'S LEGACY TO AMERICA

JOHN E. HOUSER

authorHOUSE®

AuthorHouse™
1663 Liberty Drive, Suite 200
Bloomington, IN 47403
www.authorhouse.com
Phone: 1-800-839-8640

First published by AuthorHouse 10/29/2010

ISBN: 978-1-4343-4188-4 (sc)

Printed in the United States of America
Bloomington, Indiana

This book is printed on acid-free paper.

Cover designed by
John E. Houser

But the English – ah, the English! –
they are quite a race apart.

-- Kipling

FORWARD

During the time when England was joining the European common market, I read that an Italian politician has commented that he hoped that other members would get some of what-ever-it-was that was the English. "Englishness" is something which is easily recognized though difficult to define. It occurred to me that, rather than try to draw any definition, it may be more practical to find out how they got that way.

Whatever one might think of them, everyone must recognize their accomplishments were far beyond what their number would suggest. The most obvious accomplishment has been in terms of territory, and these acquisitions were not obtained by destruction. Far more significant, however, is the gift of a common language, the first the world has had since the fall of the Roman empire. But the existence of a common language, English, demonstrates another of those contractions which occur so often during our travels through the pages of history.

This English language is a contradiction because its wide acceptance, its utility, drives some away from it. Too often we learn of groups who seek to promote a secondary language, which, while nostalgic to the proponent, can be a shackle to the pupil. While the world moves to greater, and more rapid, dissemination of information, those few who are determined to stick to another language can only retard their own abilities to participate in the constantly changing opportunities created each day.

It is worthwhile that we know the characteristics of these peoples, though we must also be aware that bearing the label 'English' is not always parochial, but may refer to the world's property. We must sort through these qualities and determine what we want to keep. If we do not, we might lose them.

I have used and abused many persons in bringing this work to fruition. I confess it was more difficult than I ever imagined. In the days when it was first taking shape, but disjointed and rambling, Daphne Flowers Wood went its entire length, questioning each thought. The Reverend Mr. Frederick A. Buechner called my hand as his conscience and training dictated. Rolf Kauka, with a historian's acumen and an internationalist's view, hammered me on the facts and my conclusions. The British Museum Library is unimaginably rich for mining of this sort. Getting in was another story, but, once in, it was of the richest seams. As I had resolved to use no source written after World War I, it may have been indispensable.

My deepest appreciation is to my wife, Rives, who read, read, and re-read this manuscript.

John E. Houser
Jacksonville, Florida

Contents

INTRODUCTION

If you were to look at a political map of the world published in the last century, you would notice that Great Britain and its Empire were customarily shown in red. If your eyes sought out this color red as it marked various areas or underlined the names of areas too small to color, you could readily see the accuracy of the saying: "The sun never sets on the British Empire." This empire included about one-fifth of both the world's people and the earth's land surface. Then should you make comparisons of those "Empire areas," together with the states fostered or developed by England, to each of their immediate neighbors, you would find those areas fostered by the English are usually better developed, or more civilized, in the sense that they are better able to cope with, and influence, their natural environments than are their neighbors. Why should this be?

The driving force of the British Empire was the English people. England, with a land area of less than 51,000 square miles, has only .00089% of the Earth's land surface. In 1940 its population was only 45 million, or .02% of the earth's total number of people. It is truly incredible that such an insignificant number of people from such a tiny homeland could have so enormous an impact. How could they do it?

One more comparison: North America was dominated by the English during its development when its character was formed. South and Central America were dominated by Latin Europeans during their development. Both these continents are remarkably similar. Both are triangular in shape. High mountains mark their western verges and lower, more inland, mountain ranges follow their eastern coasts. Both are well watered with rivers emptying into the Atlantic. Both have enough water and high enough not to be scarred by a Sahara Desert. The southern continent is to the east of its northern companion, so it should have been, and was, discovered first. Why, then, is North America more developed, more productive, and more abundant in its yield?

People are what they think. As physical beings, there is very little difference between them. What, however, occupies and travels through their minds can be, and is, vastly different. Here we shall seek to determine what is the stuff of the English mind. What are the forces that have shaped English thought? In modern terms, each mind, like a computer, has memory capacity. Our philosophy, our outlook, our religion, and our range of permissible or acceptable choices make up our "software" with which we process, evaluate, and use facts and exposures outside of our persons. What is the English matrix of thought? How did it evolve? How does it differ from that of other groups?

A person's religion defines one's duty and morality. It can impose limitations on what will be in one's inventory of thoughts. An organized religion is an instrument of limitation, and can often be one of oppression. Bertrand Russell, referring to an earlier era, said, "What is significant is that the function of religion was not conducive to the exercise of intellectual adventure." A person's duty, the willingness to do that duty, and the permissibility and drive to search for knowledge are the great variables of humankind. How does English religion treat change and inquisitiveness?

A person's habitat is of enormous importance. Those living in an area requiring all their energy merely to survive have no time to think or to improve their conditions. Where nature is harsh and unforgiving, the inhabitants' religion is filled with magic, the supernatural, and phantoms. In an unchanging desert where one's footsteps are erased as quickly as they are made, people tend to say what will be, will be.

A land of great abundance of life's needs makes nonexistent any desire for change.

What is the climate like? It affects a person's desire to work. In a hot, dry place like Spain, as in a cold country without a full day's sun, it is easy to carry over the indolence of the non-working season to that season when a product can be had. Similarly, is the locality a place of repetitive warfare? Is the community one that stays at home or is it a home of traders? Is it well watered so that crops are abundant and rivers can be highways of commerce? These are the sorts of things that affect a person's activities and the scope of that person's religion. They also affect a person's ability to cope with the rules which a religion might seek to impose. England did not come into being by itself. Indeed, everything it has and is, except the land, came from some other place. We will seek to find the seed beds from which England's ideas sprang. To understand the English, we will have to get some idea of what others were like so that we might see how the English are different. We shall try to learn how the English achieved a sense of balance.

The English attained a balance in education. An uneducated person can only express himself externally, customarily through passion or violence. On the other side, if the populous is too educated, it may become, as did ancient Greece, a nation of thinkers who rely on others to do all the physical work, feeling that other people are beneath them. To ancient Greece, a colony was simply a place to get assets for the homeland, without the need to "put anything back."

The English also achieved a balance in behavior and developed the ability to deal with others with some restraint yet some firmness too, especially so they can use the services of others to compensate for their own being so few.

Furthermore, the English achieved a balance in government. A mob is an instrument of tyranny just as is an autocracy whether of a Sovran or an aristocracy. Achieving such a balance is never admired by those on the outside and only grudgingly accepted by those within. We shall look at Britain's antecedents to get an idea of how the English obtained this balance.

What we are seeking to discover is the mental "software" that allowed so few to have so enormous an impact. What traits or thinking patterns did they possess to propagate their own image in distant areas? The United States of America, for example, was developed after the English models of law and manners which must have played an overwhelming role in its becoming a world power with a prodigious output in both agricultural and manufactured goods. Does this mean that those thinking patterns are transferable?

Because we are looking for the ingredients which molded this English character, our quest will end with the nineteenth century. Our travels into the later days, to glimpse how possessions were actually acquired or how those possessions were utilized, while not our present concern, do shed light on the sort of person whom we are studying and sometimes will confirm what we have found. Our quest, however, is to find the make-up of the people, their way of being, which made it possible that somewhere, at every hour of the day an English person stood on British soil in the full light of the day's sun. We are concerned with their religion, their philosophy, and their motivation, which were forces of enlightenment rather than instruments of oppression.

As we travel back to the very beginnings of human endeavors, we ought to remember that early man was no more equipped to face life as we know it today than the aborigine, who from time to time is "discovered," and held up for our curiosity. In those days people were organized into tribes. Those tribes probably had laws, not unlike our own, against murder, rape, or theft, but the force of those laws usually extended only to the edge of the tribe. If a tribe member took the life of someone not of that tribe, the killing was simply a thing not worthy of consideration as a wrong. If one went to another tribe, the newcomer adopted the religion of the host.

The first travels of a trader across the desert were undoubtedly guided by instinct not unlike the "navigation" of migratory birds. It is crucial to the study of history that we keep our conscience tied to what life and values were at the time of the action, and know that the progress of mankind was a slow, step by step, construction process. At first, there were no tools, and then, as now, to improve the tools, consumption had to be delayed. Then, as now, some groups resisted change and nearly everyone was fearful of it.

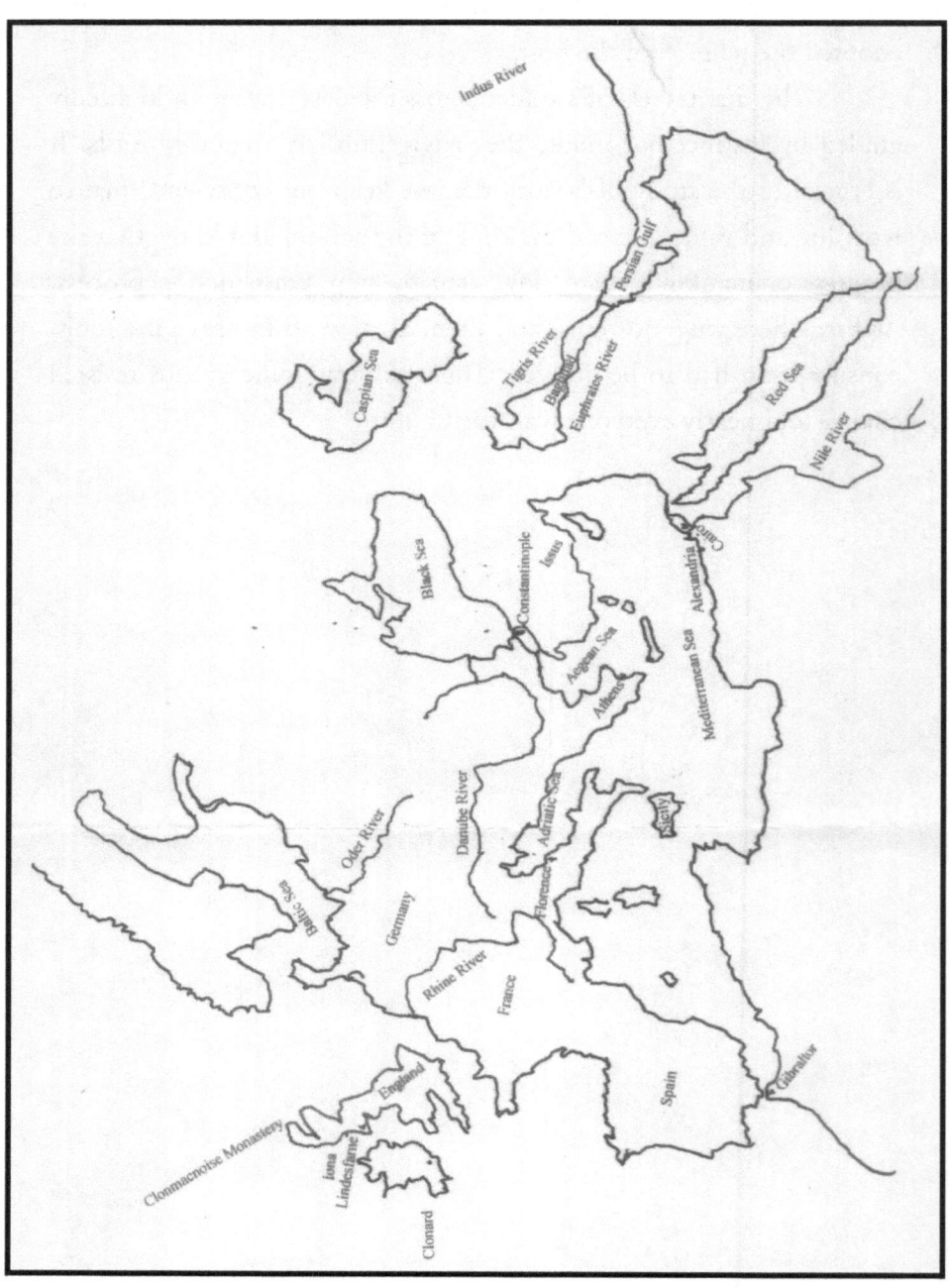

Book One

Whence the English Came

Whence the English Came

1 THE JEWISH MOTHER
*The development of a religion both portable
and independent of temporal authority.*

England's principal religious influence is within that broad, ill-defined group gathered under the term "Christianity." But Christians are oftentimes markedly different, antagonistic, and fundamentally in disagreement when they define themselves or their beliefs. Christianity, like so many plants, takes its outward form from the ground in which it grows. What is the English sort, and how does it differ from other forms of Christianity? We shall now seek to learn whence it came and how it was adapted to England. Christianity is said to have been born out of a Jewish mother, by a Greek father, and raised in a Roman nursery. This is an apt description. Of course, "Roman" in this sentence means the Roman empire and has nothing to do with the later-formed Roman church.

To find the beginnings of this Jewish mother, we must travel back to Mesopotamia where our civilization began. "Civilization" implies the ability to change one's environment, rather than to simply live in it and endure everything it dishes out. Civilized life requires an ability to engage in a cooperative effort.

Meso [between] potamia [rivers] is that area between the Tigris and Euphrates rivers in present-day Iraq. The lower parts of those rivers, where the two come together, form a valley which is a part of a great alluvial plain extending all the way to China. It was a marshy, fertile area which, through a reasonably careful effort by those living along its banks, was capable of producing a surplus of food and other crops.

To have civilization, there must be a surplus. A surplus allows people to leave their plows or spears and to live in cities and to acquire knowledge through intellectual work.

The earliest-known people of Mesopotamia were the **Sumerians**. They settled in the eastern tip of the Fertile Crescent, a quarter-moon shaped area that extended upward and over to the edge of the Mediterranean Sea. Other tribes joined the Sumerians and settled in other portions of this Crescent. These people, each with its own set of gods and customs, rubbed elbows, traded with one another, wore away old notions, and developed new ones. But their religions conflicted, and these differing beliefs could not account for the upheavals and natural calamities which occurred from time to time. From this confusion came an increasing acceptance of the notion of "monotheism," belief in one god.

As these tribes became increasingly monotheistic, each tribe dropped its special, private gods. By doing so, they resolved a host of conflicts among themselves. Equally important, as they lived near one another, they were sometimes forced to question their own customs and prohibitions. As an example, if one tribe had a prohibition against a certain food, yet its members saw their neighbor thrive on the same food, their own prohibition became suspect. And if they suffered a shortage and were forced to eat the forbidden food, they, again, must have questioned their own beliefs.

In this early period, a nomadic tribe called **Hebrews**, "wanderers," appeared. By tradition they had come out of Egypt. These Hebrews adopted the notion of monotheism and developed the idea that there was a covenant between themselves and God. They believed if they did something, God would make a response. They also developed an abstract notion of God and forbade God's representation by "graven," sculptured or engraved images. Together, these notions gave a feeling of individual accountability but made it difficult to circumscribe their god.

Rather than soothsayers or an organized group, the Hebrews had "prophets" who were poets, preachers, or critics. These prophets depended upon their own power of persuasion to act as spokespersons for God. Through prophets, the Hebrews developed high ethical standards independent of any temporal power. Indeed, it may have been the lack of any formal priestly order over the prophets which allowed them to announce such standards. It was through these ethical standards that a firm connection was made between acceptable behavior, morality, and religion. Because morality emanated from God, a king could be questioned or criticized.

In the three centuries ending with the Babylonian exile in about 600 B.C., notions of justice and redemption were developed. Isaiah and Jeremiah closed this period with their presentation of the idea of moral character coupled with certain punishment for sin. Again, this morality was not defined or constricted by any tribal or state authority.

About 600 B.C. Jerusalem was destroyed, and the Hebrews who had not previously fled were taken in bondage to Babylon. In Babylon, the captives had no temple in which to worship or make sacrifices. As a replacement, these Jewish people met in ordinary buildings which they would designate as a place of worship, a synagogue. In those buildings they developed a non-sacrificial service using a liturgy, a prescribed form of worship service. Ezekiel stressed regular Sabbath services. Jeremiah taught that God was omnipotent and His covenant was with the person and not the tribe. These important changes freed the Jewish religion of both the state and the temple. It became portable, and though not yet conceived, it could be the religion of persons other than Hebrews. "Second Isaiah" completed this concept by stating the "oneness" of God. God was universal, catholic. God was linked to righteousness, to redemption, and to joy. Linking God to joy was a new religious concept which could open untold horizons for thought. Joy was permissible.

Ironically, Judaism, which began as a tribal religion, grew so that it could embrace others. That is, the religion outgrew the tribe. Probably all religious groups accepted converts if the person were acceptable to the tribe. But this group freed its religion, first from temporal power, then from a definite place or object, and surmounted those with the notion its god was universal. It had molded for itself beliefs and precepts which mandated that its basic tenets did apply to others, and this conviction was so whether or not the regular adherents accepted it.

2 THE GREEK FATHER

The origins and scope of Grecian knowledge
and its fusion with Christianity.

All of us are familiar with painting by the numbers. As children, we had kits with an outline of a picture and a number within each of the spaces. The kit came with various colored paints, each identified with its own number. Our job was to put the paint in the spaces "by the numbers." In ancient Greece we find the people who drew the outlines of our knowledge and assigned the numbers to our skills.

Greece is a low country with gentle rivers and without insurmountable mountains. These physical characteristics gave the Greeks a feeling their homeland was a hospitable place in which to live. The Greeks were unlike others who blocked out the horrors of their homeland by flights of imagination because they did not live in places with unconquerable mountains and treacherous rivers. Rather than a great mass of superstition and frightful gods, the Greeks knew what was on the other side. They could climb their mountains and could think about what they were made of, how they were formed, and even if they might be changed to make them more useful. The Greeks gave their gods human attributes, a reflection of their lack of an overpowering fear of their surroundings. By contrast, India's folklore tells of its ancients as living for 10,000 years as a way of escaping from, or coping with, their surroundings. Likewise, the Jews suggested a life of 900 years.

Imagine having no laboratory, no microscope, no magnifying glass, and no inkling about how a tree is formed or composed. Then imagine that someone, by pure reasoning, conceives that a tree is made of minute blocks and the difference between that tree and other objects is the arrangement and compactness of the blocks which are contained in it. The people who believed that apparently silly notion were called "atomists." Then imagine not being laughed at or ridiculed for such a silly idea. This example gives us an inkling of what those Greeks were made.

They were capable of strange thoughts. What may be more remarkable is that they could tolerate those thoughts in others. In our own day how often do we adopt an intransigent position on some issue, resting on our own notions alone, refusing to brook any discussion? The Greeks liked to think. Thinking requires a certain tolerance for another's opinions. The Greeks designed and made this outline on our canvas of knowledge in the span between the lives of **Thales**, the first Greek philosopher, who died in 550 B.C. and Aristotle, who died in 322 B.C. – a mere speck of time!

The marvel of the Greeks was how they thought. With the use of axioms, logic, and contradiction, they could reason from the particular to a general principle and back to particulars. The Chinese, by contrast, were accomplished mathematicians, but they were concerned solely with the measurement of space and volume. The purpose of the Chinese was merely to adjust to the environment. They had no desire to change it as the Greeks actually did. The Hindu mind regarded the world as fixed and its people in mental strait jackets. It was such a mentality that gave birth to the caste system. Children were locked in the social standing of their parents. In those ancient days only the Greeks were able to think rationally that their circumstance could be changed by their own efforts. The Greeks thought about matter, metaphysics, and conduct. They alone, of all the ancient thinkers, felt that life was to be enjoyed and that the individual was useful and worthwhile.

The Greek method of thinking was empirical, based on experience. It grew out of the Grecian landscape which was neither forbidding nor overpowering. **Empiricism** is a concept that holds knowledge is derived from the senses. Under this concept, the mind is a blank tablet which gathers impressions from experiences to which it is exposed. As it does so, it develops an ability to "use" and correlate these data. Repetitive exposures to a same phenomenon leads one to conclude certain ideas may be "laws" from which we make other comparisons and deductions. While these "laws" may not truly be fixed principles, from their repetition, according to empiricism, they are useful to the mind to organize or correlate new sensations and perceptions it receives. Where persons in other cultures might see a raging river or a mountain reaching into the clouds and conclude their gods had made impenetrable barriers to block their path, the early empirically minded Greeks would dwell on the obstacle's characteristics as compared to other observed phenomena to understand or explain what they saw.

Plato and Aristotle

In addition to making the road map for all our quests for knowledge, the Greeks were the fathers of Christianity. The simple tribal religion of the Hebrews was merged with Greek thoughts about conduct and ethics, which later gave to Christianity a depth of meaning, a theology. This merger was based principally on the works of Plato and Aristotle, two persons, teacher and pupil, who had markedly different effects. Plato's imprint is on England. Aristotle's is on wide areas of Europe.

Plato said objects we can see or feel cannot be an ultimate reality because they are constantly changing. Neither oak trees nor oak leaves are always the same. Further, as an object can be beautiful to one person and not another, the observed "beauty" cannot be an ultimate reality. Plato reasoned that the ultimate reality of an object or a concept cannot be changeable. So these things which we experience each day are reflections of, or emanations from a "real" tree or "form" of a tree, or of "real beauty" or a "form of beauty," or of whatever we become aware. Each of these "forms" is, in turn, an emanation of a higher, or more generic, "form," continuing to the highest "form" which he called "good." This Platonic thought is a high order of empiricism as it takes what can be seen and felt, then makes conclusions about other things which the mind cannot know. And it does so without superstition.

For our purposes – and as his ideas have been applied to Western thought – Aristotle was also concerned with a hierarchy of "matter" and "form," but he tied them together more closely. He said the ultimate "form" was within the matter which we observe. Aristotle held that because the "form" was within the object, the form of that object was predetermined and fixed. As an example, because the form of "oakness" is within the acorn and the oak tree, it can only be an oak.

As applied by those coming after him, when the "central element" was discovered, Aristotelian thought held everything dependant upon that center was fixed and had to be consistent with that center. Therefore, because the highest, or ultimate, reality is known, only deductive reasoning can exist. If one can assert the central element is fixed, or known, the possible manifestations, emanations, or objects from that fixed center have to conform, and are, therefore, limited in scope. This concept of fixed result, or narrow range of results, had a profound effect upon human progress. It was the bane of Galileo and made rough waters for Darwin.

To visualize this difference, we might think of a sphere with a light inside, but with perforations and thin places on its outer shell. We wish to discover what the light and the ball are and how they are made. Since the light is on the inside, we can learn their "exact" dimensions and makeup. This is a way to think of how Aristotle's thoughts were used.

Now suppose we had another ball, but the source of its light comes from the outside. First, we must realize we see on the outside of the ball only a speck of all the light which is emanating from the source of the light. If we study an apple illuminated by light from an electric bulb, we see only the light which strikes the apple, but we know the bulb is putting out light from is entire surface. And we know the light is simply a tool to discover the makeup of the apple, but it did not put any outward boundary on what the apple, or the light, could be. Such was the Platonistic thought pattern.

Fusion of Judaism and Platonism

The fusion of Judaism and Platonism was the work of **Philo**, a Jewish thinker living in Alexandria just before the birth of Christ. Like Plato, Philo said the experienced world, always in flux, was different from the "forms." Philo recognized Plato's hierarchy of forms, but Philo said the highest was "God" and not simply "Good" as Plato had described the ultimate reality.

This joinder was the key. This was an expression of God as the ultimate reality. Religious Platonism rested upon the principles that 1) there exists a sharp distinction between God and the world; 2) no direct contact occurs between them, except through intermediaries such as a stream of light, God's ideas or words; and 3) one can know God only through mystical, intuitive, connection.

Another element of the Greek father was **gnosticism**, "knowledgeism." The gnostics felt that through knowledge, one could attain release from the body, light, and salvation. Jesus, as a light of, or to, God would fit into gnosticism, since, by study, intuitive thoughts, and mysticism, one can know, or make a connection with, God. These ideas were in harmony with one another.

The Greeks gave to mankind ways of using the mind. Their patterns, or outlines, were so broad and so accurate that today's accumulated knowledge has been acquired by the use of these Grecian models despite interludes of rejection or constriction.

3 THE ROMAN NURSERY

The breadth and strength of the Roman empire
provided Christianity a nursery and caused the
communication of Hellenic thought to Britain.

Rome under the leadership of **Augustus** was the capital of the world at the beginning of the Christian era. Rome had conquered the East, but the East just as surely had conquered Rome. The language of the educated person was Greek. Its art and its culture were taken from, or modeled after, the Greeks. Rome, in a sense, was an outpost of the Hellenic world.

In A.D. 14 Tiberius became chief of state of the Roman empire. The span from his accession through the reign of Marcus Aurelius (A.D. 161-180), was called **Pax Romana**, Roman Peace. In *The Decline and Fall of the Roman Empire*, Gibbon said of this period, "If a man were called to fix the period in the history of the world, during which the condition of the human race was most happy and prosperous, he would, without hesitation, name that which elapsed from the death of Domitian to the accession of Commodus."

In those days of the Pax Romana, Rome was unlike any city the world had known. The empire was at its greatest extent. It reached as far north as Scotland then across Europe to the northern shore of the Black Sea, continuing to the Caspian Sea and beyond to include the Tigris-Euphrates valley, around Egypt and east to the Atlantic, taking all the developed areas within its sweep. In a real sense there was nothing else of any consequence in the world.

Within this great sweep, the empire was blessed with superb harbors and efficient sea transport. Shipping was the work of private individuals or consortiums. The sea lanes and the harbors were clogged with traffic. Rome and Italy were the great importing areas. Shippers, as well as other entrepreneurs and tradesmen who served the needs of the empire, were favored and encouraged. The outer boundaries were protected by army garrisons. Army units within the empire assured the peace. While the Romans could be capable of extreme cruelty, they were tolerant as long as peace was maintained. A developed postal system extended throughout the length and breadth of the Roman empire. A traveler could go anywhere in comparative safety and, as Greek was the language of educated persons, that traveler could transact business anywhere within the empire.

At home the Romans used and abused their wealth, and kept the appearance of a constitutional government with the image of a ruling senate. Rome was the center of power. A network of aqueducts supplied water throughout the city. Baths were built for the relaxation and amusement of its citizens. Grand public buildings abounded. Its markets were filled with fresh foods and luxuries from every part of the world. Some of its people accumulated vast personal wealth. Sporting events were regularly organized for the pleasure of everyone. A private banking system provided a ready means for the flow of this enormous wealth. All the symbols of these great riches were repeated in cities across the reach of Roman arms.

Rome never rivaled Athens as a center of learning and thought, but if there were new ideas, they were brought to Rome. The Romans knew of all the great thoughts by the Greeks. They knew that **Ptolemy** proved the world was round. They were aware of the various schools of philosophy. **Pliny** defended Rome's place in the intellectual world by saying the "immense majesty of the Roman peace" caused the diffusion of knowledge.

Among all the wares and ideas brought to Rome were a number of Eastern mystery religions. Christianity and Mithraism were probably the most widespread, though they were simply two among many, each of which had its own cult or sect. At the same time, Rome, of course, had its own Hellenized religion, which increasingly included the emperor. These eastern religions, as other religions, were tolerated until persecutions were begun under Nero.

Rome's philosophy was **Stoic**. Plato and Aristotle had thought of the "good life" as being a citizen of the city-state. Their secondary concern was of the individual, but the individual was always to act with great self-control. When Alexander defeated the city-states of Greece, the Greek thinkers had to find something other than the state which would be a "constant" as an anchor for their faith. Some become "epicureans," believing sensual and bodily pleasures to be the good life. Another group developed the idea of "stoicism." They thought of themselves as citizens of the world. They believed in the universality of god and the brotherhood of man. They saw god and nature as good. "Evil" existed only if one thought it existed. There was good in everything. A person had simply to find it. The Stoics thought that each person must strive to overcome passion and emotion, because passion was what led people to see evil. They were very cosmopolitan, urbane, public-spirited people. Their thoughts were ideal for an empire. Emphasis was shifted to the individual rather than to a tribe or state.

A growing force was the philosophy of **Neo-Platonism**, a synthesis of all the Greek philosophers, including Plato, Aristotle, and the Greeks living in Alexandria during the third century. Its tendency was to explain ultimate phenomena or reality on a mystical (intuitive) basis. **Plotinus** was a principal thinker of this group. Later it was often given over to theurgy, or divine intervention, but, for our concerns, it remained a valid synthesis of Grecian philosophy which can be harmonious with Christianity. Plato, we recall, said the natural things of this world were a reflection or emanation of a series of "ideas" or "forms" until one reached the highest "form" which Plato called "Good" and Philo of Alexandria had called "God." This concept was then blended with Stoicism, making it all-embracing and centered on the individual. Later this mixture was blended into Christianity.

Plato used the sun as one of his illustrations which was readily adapted to religious Neo-Platonism. From the sun comes light and heat, yet, for all that constant supply, the sun does not wear out. Without it there is total darkness. It is not part of the world, but the world could not exist without it. We can only know about the sun by what it does. We can not even look at it. Clearly, this example can be a way of thinking of God: not of this world, but indispensable to it, yet unknowable except intuitively, mystically.

In the Platonic and Neo-Platonic mode of thinking, all the "boundaries" of human thought, if there be any, are beyond what the senses can know. Those boundaries are outside the ball. And thought is "illuminated" by forces separate from the realm of the perceivable. Thomas Jefferson aptly defined thought as "the illimitable freedom of the human mind." This philosophical basis, as we have seen, was combined with "knowledgeism" to hold that the result of accumulated knowledge can provide, and it is permissible that it provide, a better life,

The Origin of British Christianity

Christianity, dressed in all this Grecian garb, travelled along with the army and persons of trade throughout the furthermost reaches of the empire. In A.D. 43 the empire was extended to Britain and the Celts. The Britons, in their "granary of the north," received all the benefits of empire, including Christianity which came as part of the baggage.

The earliest liturgy used in England is thought to have been Gallican and that it had been introduced into Gaul near the beginning of the second century by missionaries from Asia Minor. The liturgy used in England during the Roman occupation has been lost, but there is virtual identity of the Eucharistic service in the ancient Gallic liturgy as compared with that in use in England in 1900. Bede tells us in *A History of the English Church and People* that upon his own written request, in A.D. 167 King **Lucius** was baptized as a Christian. In A.D. 314 the British, the Celtic church, sent three bishops to a council in Arles, and in A.D. 400, the Celtic monk **Pelagius** arrived in Rome to start a firestorm about clerical abuses. In A.D. 410 the Romans withdrew from Britain.

Both Rome and the Romans who settled in Britain were very different when the Romans left the island, never to return, 400 years later. **Diocletian** (245-313) had reorganized the empire to stem the tide of losses to the barbarians. He divided the Empire into eastern and western provinces, and those were further subdivided into districts which he called "dioceses," with each governed by a "vicar." Rome ceased to be the seat of government. It was moved first to Milan then to Ravenna.

Constantine, whose mother, by legend, was the daughter of a British prince, issued the Edict of Milan in A.D. 313. Through this pronouncement Christians were permitted to worship freely. In A.D. 330 he moved the capital of the empire to the shores of the Bosporus and renamed his capital city Constantinople. When he left Italy, Latins lost their special status, and Rome became merely a shell of its former self. Where previously all the new ideas had been brought to Rome, they were taken to Constantinople. Only the Latins remained.

Such was the nursery in which Christianity grew and took its first steps. In the first years of Christianity, Rome was wealthy. It kept intact a pretense of democratic rule through its senate. Until the third century, Greek was taught in schools throughout the empire. While not possessed of great thinkers who made lasting achievements, Rome had sufficient ability and riches, with a common language, to distribute the available knowledge to all its provinces. Ideas rubbed together, and blended, softened, and some of the rough edges were worn away. After Constantine issued his Edict of Milan, Christianity became the dominate eastern mystery religion. It had learned to speak with a Greek tongue, lived in a Grecian culture, and thought with a Grecian mind.

Ancient Rome's development of this oriental mystery religion, with its marriage to Greek philosophy and its examples of practical politics and statecraft, is Rome's great legacy to the modern world.

4 AFRICANIZING OF THE CHRISTIAN CHURCH IN ROME

The westward migration of Asiatic thought
patterns from the Near East along the African
coast, coupled with the decline of Rome
caused a decline of intellectual growth.

To this point in our journey we have seen a blending of influences, each unlike the other but somehow compatible. As Rome's strength declined, an entirely new, but vastly different, force came to that city. profoundly affecting a great portion of the Christian church, and, consequently, western thought. What was it? Where did it come from?

Phoenician Traditions

The **Phoenicians**, a branch of the Semite family who pursued that most un-Semitic of trades, seamanship, began in ancient Sidon and Tyre, on the Syrian coast. Trade took them to Sicily and along the African coast from Libya through the Pillars of Hercules, Gibraltar, and into the Atlantic. They are thought to be the ones who gave us an alphabet, an indispensable tool for trade.

The Phoenicians were a greedy lot, yet they were the only ones who always had trading privileges in Egypt. The Greeks did not like them, but were dependent upon them. For example, the fir for Solomon's temple was supplied by the Phoenicians. Their trade with the Arabs was uninterrupted. They were the envy of all who plied the seas as they were navigators without peer. They knew the winds, the currents, and the tides, and they kept their knowledge of seamanship to themselves.

The trade beyond Gibraltar was a Phoenician monopoly. Their commerce carried them to Sierra Leone in the south and to the north shores of Europe and to Britain, though no one had yet invented the compass. Their trade with Spain was so lucrative that their vessels returned with silver anchors. Few commodities entered into the stream of commerce that were not carried in Phoenician bottoms.

The Phoenician cities of Sidon and Tyre had been overrun by the Macedonians who founded **Alexandria** in 332 B.C. at the mouth of the Nile. Alexandria became the seaport for the eastern end of the Mediterranean. Tyre and Sidon never revived, but further to the west, the Phoenicians had settled the cities of Hippo, Utica, and **Carthage**. Carthage was destined to surpass them all.

Carthage was an aristocratic city based on wealth rather than birth. Its favorable location allowed it to surpass the greatness of Sidon and Tyre. Carthage grew rich through its domination of the trade to the west, and by transforming north Africa into a garden paradise. For Carthage, and later for Rome, the African coast was a fertile garden of irrigated vineyards and plantations of lush abundance. **Scipio Africanus**, the Roman general who conquered Carthage, was lavish in his praise of her agriculture.

The Semitic race, who included these Carthaginians, claimed commerce and trade as their field of mastery, while the Greeks, Romans, and Germans of the Indo-European race claimed heroism, art, and legislation as their genius. The business of the Carthaginians was commerce. They could express the value of everything and everyone in terms of money. As merchants in a state resting it laurels on those who succeeded in trade and commerce, they celebrated and encouraged the trader's mind. Theirs was a mind and an ethic which stressed the practical, the mechanical resolution of concerns, so that transactions could be completed. Such solutions were important to them as oftentimes they dealt with persons with whom they would have no other contact. This was not a society given to philosophy or to mental ruminations. Their minds were precise, arithmetically correct, and authoritarian. They sought to resolve differences to facilitate trade. They did not want controversy or lengthy explanations, but rather only practical and direct solutions. Equally, theirs was not a mind interested in art, as art is impractical.

In 146 B.C. Rome defeated Carthage. These Phoenicians of North Africa, from Libya westward through Mauritania and beyond Gibraltar, became a part of the Roman empire. When Christianity later came to Carthage, its route was from Sicily, a land of kindred Semites. The Christianity which came to Carthage was moving into, and among, the minds of traders.

Surprisingly, and unlike Rome, Latin – not Greek – was the language used in the African Christian church. **Tertullian**, an early bishop of Carthage, was the first writer of any consequence to compose Christian writings in Latin, and **Augustine of Hippo**, a fellow African, learned about Christianity through the writings of Tertullian. Consequently, as the African church grew, it rapidly took on its own gloss from both the Africans' own way of thinking and from the use of a different language. It was not long before the African church expressed its resentment of Rome. In A.D. 225 a church council meeting in Carthage prohibited appeals of religious questions to Rome. Again in A.D. 411 a council meeting in Carthage adopted a canon which read "whoever appeals to a court on the other side of the sea may not again be received into communion with anyone in Africa."

Movement had always been free within the empire, and as the Roman court left Rome, the Africans moved in. The native Latin, who suddenly was the predominant element after the capital of the empire was moved to the east, was a practical sort of person, but not brilliant. The Latins' new companions were persons of commerce.

Within slightly more than 100 years after Constantinople was dedicated as the new capital of the Roman empire in 330, the African church, with its Latin language, had superseded the church of Rome. Leo I was elected pope in 440, and though he is not thought to have been the first pope born in Rome, he was the first celebrated preacher to use the Latin language. This sect of the Christian community got a new drummer, and it was dressed in the mental garb of the practical and the authoritarian. The Christian church in Rome was no longer a Hellenistic, Neo-Platonistic religion, but was instead charting a new course that was interested in the affairs of state as well as those of the spirit.

When the Africans took over the church in Rome, change followed rapidly and decisively. Though the emperor in Constantinople asserted authority over all western territories, including Rome, his ability to enforce his edicts grew weaker because the empire was constantly under pressure from barbarians along its northern frontier. The new church in Rome took to itself the reins of authority whenever they were released by others.

The Roman bishop claimed for himself the exclusive right to use the title of pope. The first, it is thought, to have made this claim was Celestine I (422-432). "Patriarch" was the title used by the first bishops in the sees created by the apostles. In the beginning, "pope" was widely used by clerics, but today only the Roman bishop uses that title in the West, while many clerics use it in the Orthodox churches.

Leo I (440-461) is regarded by some as the founder of the medieval papacy because he asserted, then enforced, the monarchical idea that the bishop in Rome was over the other bishops. The original idea was "first among equals" (*episcopus inter episcopos*) but Celestine, without precedent, asserted that he was over other bishops (*episcopus episcoporum*). Leo augmented this with his theory of "Petrine supremacy," which held that as Peter was the rock upon which the church was founded, Rome, his see, was of first dignity. Such a theory, however, should seem to suggest Jerusalem as foremost. **Gelasius** (492-496) was the first Roman bishop to declare the papacy to be independent of both the state and church councils in matters of faith. **Gregory I** (590-604) was the bishop who cast these notions in concrete. These ideas of supremacy first extended to Italian bishops, and gradually they were expanded to include virtually all other European bishoprics. The Roman church, with its own constitution, laws, and succession, was developing a life of its own, independent of any state: an emerging theocracy. As Creighton would later say, "not a church at all, but a state in its organization, and the worst kind of state, an autocracy."

These newcomers from Africa recognized the need for a history and an organization, but there was none, nor could there have been. After the systematic persecutions of Christians began, especially in the reign of Valerian (253-259), to have an organization with written records would have been tantamount to issuing warrants for the arrest of Christians. It must follow that, very little, if anything, is known of the earliest Roman bishops. Their identities, if indeed they existed, may be entirely fictitious. What the new Afro-Roman church could not establish, it filled in so that the line of Roman bishops is uninterrupted from the Apostle Peter. All the records of this period were written centuries later.

This Afro-Roman church adopted Roman titles such as "pontiff," "pontifax maximus," "pius," and "father." The church used Roman divisions of "dioceses" under the charge of a "vicar." It accepted the Grecian custom of deifying mortals and made saints of those on its own list of Roman bishops. The Afro-Roman church worked efficiently in a manner consistent with its trader origins.

Germanic Invaders and the New Roman Church

The Germanic invaders had no feelings for Rome or its empire, so as the Roman empire crumbled, this Afro-Roman church grew. As we have mentioned, the removal of the seat of government from Rome was concurrent with Germanic pressure from the north. A number of these Germanic invaders were **Arian Christians**, and their dispute was with the Roman government, but not with the church in Rome. Arian Christianity came to the Franks and other Germanic tribes through **Ulfilas** (c. 311-385) who is said to have devised a Gothic alphabet then translated the Bible from Greek to Gothic. The Germanic invaders, like others, were often intrigued by the pomp and showmanship of the Roman church. And remember also many of them were like children in a candy store, wanting that which Rome represented, while putting their hands all over the showcase. The Roman church was a way to get the reward without bowing to the owner. In 496 the Franks were converted to the religion of the church of Rome.

The sources of the Rhine and the Danube Rivers are quite close together. The Rhine flows to the Atlantic while the Danube flows to the Black sea. Germanic tribes had been pushed westward out of Asia by the **Huns**. By the fourth century, the Germans were generally north of the Rhine-Danube line and the Romans were south of it. When they first arrived, the Germanic peoples could be likened to the American Indians at the time when the Europeans came to North America. These Germans were bright people who learned from the Romans through trade with them, and later, while serving as their border garrisons.

The **Huns** were quite different from the other barbarians pressing on the northern borders. They were described by Ammianus Marcellinus in his *Roman History* as coming from somewhere vaguely out of the frozen lands beyond the Sea of Azov. They had faces scarred from gashes at birth, thick necks, and powerful limbs, so they resembled two-legged beasts. They wore clothing of linen which was never washed or changed but worn until it fell off in shreds. Their shoes were so crudely made they had difficulty walking, so they were called "people who trip up while walking." Their food, mostly wild roots and meat, was never cooked or seasoned, but Ammianus records it was "warmed a little" by putting in on the backs of their horses and sitting on it as they rode. They roamed at large, inured from infancy to cold, thirst or famine. They had no structures of any kind, fearing to be indoors. The Huns lived and slept on their horses, even sitting sidesaddle to do their chores. Their women lived on wagons where procreation and birthing and everything else was done. They had no regular leader and gave only irregular obedience to anyone. In battle they rushed in as a group armed with only swords and lassos used to trip their enemy after a fusillade of arrows. Then they would break into small bands, hit hard and fast, and disappear. They were quarrelsome, volatile, deceitful, without any notions of right and wrong, and without any religion.

With their faces pressed against the glass of civilization, the Germans, together with Gothic, and later the Hunnic tribes, began crossing that Rhine-Danube line to strike at the western portions of the Empire. As these groups carved up the empire, the Roman church sought each tribe as members and remained aloof from political disputes except those which could affect that church's interests.

The Birth of Feudalism

Constant warfare by these Germanic tribes, first with the old Roman empire, then with anyone in Europe, made people flee to the protection of feudalism. Equally, the Roman church made and broke alliances as easily as any civil ruler, being partner or foe as its own interests dictated. The church afforded great opportunity to the ordinary person who chose to become a cleric. He could obtain an education with a change to rise to great heights. On the other hand, the effect of the medieval church was disastrous as it condemned others to the church-sanctioned slavery of feudalism.

At the beginning of the Middle Ages after the fall of Rome, the center of population in Europe was slowly moving north of the Alps. But the ordinary person was locked by poverty into the double vises of church and civil autocracy. Because the soil north of the Alps is heavy, while to the south it was light and easy to till, farming was unproductive until a plow could be invented and a proper harness could be rigged so that draft animals could pull in tandem. As a consequence, any economic impetus for relief was to be in the distant future.

The Beginning of the Dark Ages

The practical, trading background of the Afro-Latinized church of Rome was most devastating in the field of education. Augustine's City of God idealized the notion of an absolute monarchy. The Roman church cast itself in that role. His dictum implied total acceptance of church authority. As a handmaiden to this physical absolutism, uncompromising acceptance of church dogma was required with thought given only to concepts emanating from church "truths." If reason collided with church doctrines, reason had to be abandoned. A student could make observations – though not of nature – but only to give added confirmation of church dogma and doctrine. Again, if the source of light is inside the ball, the ball and its holes and thin places are measurable and known. Obviously, a thought inconsistent with the known light source or ball perforations was incorrect. This absolutism is confirmed by **Giorgio Vasari**, writing in *Lives of the Artists* in the sixteenth century, that Pope **Gregory I** issued an edict against all the remaining sculpture and works of art which had not been stolen or destroyed.

Neo-Platonism, the dominant philosophy of the late empire, was replaced by pagan-like feelings of fear and rigidity. Augustine of Hippo gave this expression with his dogma: We should believe that we might know. This is a complete reversal of knowledge for its own sake. This ultimate subordination of free inquiry was a weapon in the church's arsenal for a theocratic state. From the fall of Rome in 410 to the reign of Charlemagne, virtually all inquiry was effaced from the European mind until the Renaissance. The Platonic love of knowledge, *libido sciendi*, was replaced by the scholastic love of ignorance, ama nescire, but finally overcome in the Renaissance. As Immanuel Kant expressed in 1784: *"Sapere aude!* Dare to know! Have the courage to use your own understanding; this is the motto of the Enlightenment." Descartes had earlier expressed this notion: *"Ego cogito, ergo sum"* – I think; therefore, I am. It is sad, but a recurring truth, that a new religion moving into inadequately civilized peoples affects the accuracy of their histories and the range of their thoughts. As examples of the injury done by priests of the Roman church to Welsh and Irish history see Pritchard's *Researches into the Physical History of Mankind.*

During the early Middle Ages, study of the ancient writings was almost nonexistent with only writing drills by clerics of the Roman church, except, as we will see, that which remained in the care of the Celtic church in Ireland. The first effort to restore enlightenment was the **Carolingian Renaissance**, during the reign of the German, Charles the Great, **Charlemagne**. Its guiding hand was the Englishman Alcuin of York, who was commissioned by Charlemagne to create schools. Alcuin had been trained in the Celtic tradition of the British church, and was known as "the most learned man of his age." Alcuin copied, or had copied, the manuscripts of the Celtic church to serve as the nucleus of his library in France. Charlemagne had the rich and lively Germanic tales recorded, though tragically, they have been lost. Only his collection of Germanic laws survived. Legend holds that Fredegarius Scholasticus is also thought to be a compiler of Frankish legends. Some of these events occurred as late as 637, so it is difficult to ascribe a date to such a writer, if he be a single person.

The next attempt to rekindle the light of knowledge was by Charles the Bald through the services of the Englishman **John Scotus Erigena**, but that also failed with the coming of the Norseman.

Vulgate Latin was the only written language allowed by the Roman church, but the people spoke and thought in other tongues; consequently, this entire period, outside the sway of the Celts, is wanting for anything of literary consequence until Dante and Chaucer. How could an aspiring poet or storyteller record feelings in a foreign language?

With all these forces acting in unison, there is little wonder that the Age of the Ancients is over and the Dark Age has begun. The gift to mankind of the ancient Greeks was the knowledge that man could affect his environment and change the circumstances of his life; he need not simply accept his lot on earth. These Carthaginians and Latins, with their progeny who had assumed the authority of the Christian church in Rome, made Scripture, as read by them, the immutable control over man's destiny on earth.

European history is a sad tale of constant killings among a succession of Merovingians, Carolingians and other passing rulers, who all, except Charlemagne and Charles the Bald, were soaking in the numbing brine of theocratic ignorance made rigid by feudalism. After Leo, with the exception of Gregory, the Roman church was bereft of papal talent. These were horrid times.

Before we leave this wretched era of constant warfare and ordained ignorance, we need to throw in another handful of discord, but one which will eventually make a cold frame for new seedlings of enlightenment.

The Donation of Pepin

Pepin III, or Pippin, (714?-768) the father of Charlemagne, ruled while the Roman papacy was at a very low ebb. The eastern emperor was still Sovran of the Roman pope, though, admittedly, he had no real strength to enforce his authority. The Lombards came out of Prussia and occupied present-day Lombardy. These Lombards challenged the very foundations of the papacy. They had laid siege to Rome, and the pope asked for Pepin's assistance. Pepin responded by recapturing the former imperial lands held by the Lombards. He presented the pope those lands, the so-called "Donation of Pepin." This "gift" was the beginning of the papal states. The mere existence of the papal states kept the Italian peninsula cut up into a number of individual states or principalities that fought among themselves, each becoming a fortress.

We close this period with the Italian peninsula and the Teutonic lands north of the Alps cut into small political subdivisions. France, though calling itself a single state, was divided between its royal family and its nobility. Spread as a thick salve over all is a church imposing ignorance and submission, a church equally manipulative as the worst of them. The Vulgate Latin of the Roman church, rather than classical Latin, had supplanted Greek as the language of the educated person. Perhaps the churchmen were the only ones able to write. Vulgate Latin severed any remaining link to classical scholarship.

The occupation of western man was increasingly reduced to an effort to survive. Even charity was redefined from something to assist those in need to a self-centered expiation from one's own faults. Its corollary held that the use of the charitable gift, the item given, was of no concern to the giver; rather, it was solely the province of the Roman church.

5   THE RETURN OF KNOWLEDGE
TO THE WEST

Alexander's spread of Hellenic knowledge through
Asia, where it was both destroyed and nurtured by
the Islamic peoples and finally brought to Spain.

Except for the candle of the Celtic church, Grecian knowledge was snuffed out in Europe. During the Dark Ages, Greek was a dead language. Latin remained, but as it was in a vulgate form, the classics could not be truly comprehended, especially without their Greek antecedents. The Dark Age was a time of the suppression of knowledge. The Roman church had applied its own gloss to the Bible. The Italians had been drained of their capacities to learn, and the Germans were emerging from barbarism. The ones with authority had no capacity, or need, for disquieting intellectualism. How did the light return? We must return to the ancient world.

Macedonia lay just to the north of Greece. Phillip, King of the Macedons, defeated the Greek city-states, but like the Romans in later days, the Greeks defeated the Macedons culturally and intellectually. Phillip's son, **Alexander**, was schooled by Aristotle, and though given an earthly span of but thirty-three years, earned, as no other, the appellation "Great." Alexander had an prodigious appetite for knowledge. He was a natural military leader with an uncanny ability to have his troops where others never imagined they could be. He executed an astute combination of horrible cruelties and overwhelming magnanimity to defeat and intimidate his enemies.

Alexander ruled a mere thirteen years beginning in 336 B.C. In 334 he crossed the Hellespont, the Dardanelles. He defeated the Persians at the Battle of Issus, 333, reduced Tyre, and founded

Alexandria near the mouth of the Nile. In 331 he left Egypt, again defeated the Persians, conquered Babylon, and headed south to Persia. He then travelled northwest to the edge of Turkey, east near the Caspian Sea, on to Bactria, to Kabul, in and out of the Pamir Mountains, down the Indus River, and along the line of the Arabian Sea and Persian Gulf back to Babylon, where he died.

The Role of Women

Along that route, Alexander founded cities, had his officers marry into the local families, treated the people well, and made deposits of Greek knowledge throughout the length and breadth of his conquests. The early Greek writings, such as the Homeric poems, demonstrate women had an honored place in society and were treated with all respect. Such an attitude continued in Sparta, but by the seventh century B.C., wars and Asiatic influence had reduced the role of women. By 500 B.C. the woman's place was quite suppressed. In the Greek republic at the time of the Macedonian invasions, individual homes were small and dark, and woman were customarily confined to those houses while men debated in a public square. Alexander changed the Grecian life to fit that of Macedonia so that women were restored to full participation in the life of the cities. In Antioch and Alexandria, two cities established by Alexander, women were very active and fully participating citizens. When Rome was a republic, women were regularly admitted to schools and attended public affairs. Under the imperial government, women were just as loose and debauched as men. When the Roman government left Rome and the Afro-Roman church assumed power, women were reduced to a subservient role consistent with Asiatic tradition. Augustine and Jerome were especially convinced woman was a "weaker vessel."

The later-formed Roman Empire in the East, Byzantium, as it came to be known, increasingly resembled an oriental satrapy and continually fought for its survival. In fact, if not in name, Byzantium lost its power over Rome and the West by A.D. 410, losing its ability to communicate Grecian knowledge, and the West had lost its appetite for it.

Mohammed was born in **Mecca** five years after the death of Justinian in A.D. 565. Until then, Arabs had been nomadic tribesmen. Tribal influence was the strong element in their lives, with religion simply a support of tribal authority. A person was measured by his courage, loyalty, and generosity. By the seventh century, Mecca, a growing trade center, brought intensifying contacts with outsiders, thus weakening tribal ties. Their religion was increasingly irrelevant. Judaism and Christianity were considered foreign, so Mohammed and his religion were timely arrivals.

When Mohammed was about 40 years of age, he began receiving "recitations," the Koran, from God. He asserted these were from a source outside of himself and he was simply a voice. The messages were disjointed, fragmentary, without any time sequence, and each "chapter" dealt with many subjects. His preaching was based upon these "recitations," this Koran, as he received them. He claimed he was the final prophet. His teachings began to take hold and then burned their way through the Arab world as if they were a grass fire. Within 100 years Islam had spread to the Indus River, north to Samarkand, to all of Persia and Armenia, to the Black Sea, along the south coast of the Mediterranean Sea, all of the Arabian peninsula and North Africa, as well as into Spain and southern France. Its tenets were simple: Belief in Allah, in his prophet Mohammed, in his revealed word, and in resurrection and predestination. Among Islam's duties was the Holy War, the *jihad*, for spreading the faith.

Mohammedism, in its pure form, was the death knell to learning. It held that God knows best what is. The will of Allah accounts for everything. Since it is Allah's will, nothing can be done about it. Why struggle? Islam expressed the resignation of facing an empty desert. And because the Koran lacks conventional narrative sequence, logic was a concept entirely alien to the true Moslem mind. Legend said that Omar burned the books or the Alexandria library to warm the Moorish baths. The legend continued that such was the volume of works that, when distributed to 4000 baths within the city, it required six months to burn them all. He was supposed to have said, "If these writings of the Greeks agree with the book of God (Koran), they are useless and need not be preserved; if they disagree, they are pernicious, and ought to be destroyed." Of similar effect was the statement of Augustine of Hippo: "God and the soul, is there anything more? No, nothing." This was the attitude of the Islamic mind. This is quite similar to "scholasticism" of the Latin church as both held that fixed principles were uppermost and observations or thoughts had to conform to those rigid basic notions.

As this religion grew, it assimilated any cultural or ethnic group in its path, just as Christianity had done before it. Many who accepted it did so to escape the oppression of whatever yoke they might then have been under. Surprisingly, it is within this desert of thought that we find rich oasis bearing the lush fruits of knowledge.

The Return of Knowledge

The **Abbasid Caliphate** began in 750. Some of the caliphs of this dynasty are among the great names of civilization. These caliphs encouraged the rebirth of inquiry with the translation of Hindu scientific works into Arabic. Included among these works were writings on glass blowing, the making of alcohol, refining of metal, and production of gunpowder. These writings formed the nucleus of a school of chemistry.

Al-Mamun, Mamun the Great, caliph from 813 until 833, had his capital in Baghdad. In his city he organized a **House of Science** in which he systematically collected Greek, Sanskrit, Syriac, and Persian writings, much of which was embedded with Hellenism because Alexander had planted these seeds during his conquests, and because the Syriac Christian church had been able to survive. Al-Mamun had these writings translated into Arabic. The works of Plato, Aristotle, Galen, Hippocrates, Ptolemy, Euclid, Apollonius, and works on medicine are examples of the captured treasures. **Baghdad** became the intellectual capital of the world with free expression and unfettered research. This was the era of The Arabian Nights. Persons of any origin and of any religious belief were accepted. When this dynasty fell and the successors adopted the rigidity of Islam, happily for us, the **Fatamids of Cairo** established a **House of Knowledge** in 995.

While the West was plunged into the void of the Dark Ages, the Arabian world flourished, assimilating and using all the knowledge of Ancient Greece and the East. The Arabs devised the system of numerals which we use today, and with it, put mathematics on a sound basis. They invented algebra and geometry. They were masters of chemistry and freed it of magic. Foremost they recovered and preserved the great philosophic works of Greece, which they translated into Arabic, the form in which these works returned to Europe. Ibn Sina, whose Latin name was **Avicenna**, and who died in 1037, restated Aristotle, albeit from a Neo-Platonistic perspective.

This recaptured ancient knowledge returned to the west by several routes. The Venetian traders played a part, as did **Frederick II**, Holy Roman Emperor and King of the Kingdom of the Two Sicilies. But the high road was through Spain under the Moors.

Spain was an inhospitable place. It had high, arid plains cut by rivers too steep and too swift for navigation. Spaniards lived along these rivers and the small plains they afforded, but were intolerant of those along the next river; consequently, they were easy prey to every group who passed through.

The Moors in Spain

The **Moors** made Spain productive. They controlled the rivers and irrigated the land, transforming it into a lush garden never equalled before or since. The Moors absorbed the writings of the Greeks, as expanded by other Islamic guardians, and used them, and important to us, they allowed these writings to be translated into Latin. They added their own studios to this body of knowledge and augmented it further through tolerance of others. The Jews, for example, may have had as comfortable and as safe a home in Islamic Spain as at any place on earth.

By the tenth century a small army of foreigners, eager to know, came to Spain. Two of the principal translators of this wealth of knowledge to Latin were **Michael Scot**, a Scotsman who studied at Oxford, and **"Alfred the Englishman,"** papal legate to Henry III. **Adelard of Bath** was the translator of Euclid into Latin.

Gerbert, who was elected pope in 999 under the name of **Silvester II**, studied in Spain. He introduced Arabic numerals to the West. His knowledge, gleaned from the Moors, was considered so prodigious as to be supernatural. He whetted the appetite of others and the traffic continued, coming from all the western countries. Mathematics, astronomy, architecture (including the gothic style), and medicine, as well as philosophic and literary works, flowed across Europe and to England. In his *Historie de Mathematiques*, Montucla put it this way:

> [T]he Arabs were long the sole depositories of learning, and that it is to their commerce we owe the first rays of light which came to chase away the darkness of the

eleventh, twelfth, and thirteenth centuries." Of his own discipline he added that "during this period, all who obtained the greatest reputation in mathematics had been to acquire their knowledge amongst the Arabs.

Spain was the place to study medicine. The Arabs had discovered surgical techniques far beyond those of the Greeks and added a vast new knowledge of pharmacy. Jewish doctors, so renowned for their skills in the medical arts, were schooled in Spain, then practiced their skills in the courts of Europe.

Indeed, "the nations of Europe," as Bailly wrote to Voltaire, "after having grown old in barbarism, were only enlightened by the invasion of the Moors and the arrival of the Greeks." The Arabs restored to Europe a knowledge of ancient Grecian scholars whose very names, and all their works, had been almost totally erased from the European conscience.

Thus we see one of history's great contradictions: Islam was a religion of absolutes. Allah had given all the answers. To try to add to Allah's pronouncements was foolish; to contradict them was folly. Yet within this barren desert there was a string of oasis where the caravan of knowledge could be refreshed and renewed. When the Abbasid Caliphate of Baghdad reverted to true Islam, the Fatamids of Egypt were ready to receive the camel train. When it was no longer welcomed, and this caravan was required to return to the desert, the Abbasids in Spain gave hospitality to the camels bearing knowledge. Spain, too, was to fold its tents to learning, but by that time, the West was of a different spirit and had eagerly received the bright light of classical knowledge enriched by the Arabs.

6 THE RENAISSANCE AND THE REFORMATION

The twin struggles in Europe to reclaim Greek
knowledge and to break the suppressing
hold of the western Christian church.

The death knell of the Dark Ages was heralded by the ferociously cruel thunderclap of the Crusades (1096-1291), as senseless and as vicious a bloodletting as has ever been recorded in all the annals of human history. The most pernicious of all was the Children's Crusade. Children were sent to overcome the infidels on the theory that, as children, they would be untainted with sin. Few completed the journey to the East. Along the way they died of starvation and disease. Those who got to the land of the unbelieving were killed or sold into slavery.

Passions were so high during these grotesque times that the crusaders attacked any group along the way who were suspected of any deviation from the strict dictates of their church. Hordes of French were killed and maimed by these "warriors" on their way to the East. The rape of the Christians in Byzantium, who had prayed for their release by the crusaders, is a horrid burn on the Christian carpet.

The only rewards of the Crusades other than driving the Moors from Spain were strictly unintended: they broke the back of its sponsors, the Roman church. The Crusades killed so many Westerners that the very fabric of society was wrenched apart. The wars introduced Westerners to luxuries and new ideas so that they would never again be content to be locked in a mental iron maiden. The Crusaders taught the Europeans how to make gunpowder, and the Crusaders brought back the Black Death. These rewards sound as if they were penances, but in those days, and in that climate, they were prizes.

Another of history's contradictions is that the German King Otto I (912-973) was made Holy Roman Emperor with the blessing of the papacy, yet this unholy alliance meant these two officials constantly fought and neither had any real authority over Germany. In France, the French king, to gain authority at home, gave up power to the papacy and the cleric became a dominant force in that country. The papacy supported French claims against the Germans and the Holy Roman Emperor. As a result, what little semblance of a unified state that existed in France was under the tripartite heel of the Roman church, a feudal baron, and a sovran. Meanwhile, Germany, ruled by a Holy Roman Emperor, was incapable of even a pretense of statehood.

The light of knowledge could be brought to the door of the West, but its unhappy circumstance would suggest that the light would not be welcomed. The West had to be made ready to receive it, and then it had to learn how to live with it.

British Knowledge Makes Europe Receptive to Knowledge

The warm glow of the Celtic night light reached deep into the Italian peninsula and kept it ready for the return of Grecian knowledge. In *The Golden Age of the Medici*, Brinton spoke with these words:

> The Romantic poetry of Italy, 'Commedia del Arte,' came out of the national genius of her people, derived from two main sources, the Carolingian and Arthurian legends – in both cases the legend of great mythical kings who fought against heathen invasion. That of King Arthur was entwined with the individual stories of the Knights of his Round Table, and the romance of Lancelot, of Guinevere and Elaine: that of the

great King Charlemagne with his famous Paladins, Orlando, Ruggiero, Astolfo, and with the tragic issue of the great battle among the mountains in the valley of Roncesvalle. To the nobles in Italy the Arthurian legend, with its vivid picture of feudal manners and its enthralling love interest, was especially attractive: but to the people themselves the Carolingian epic, the figures of the great Christian King and his Paladins, and, above all, Orlando, the heroic Count, overwhelmed at last through treason in the dolorosa valle, the pass of Roncesvalle, was of supreme attraction, and formed the groundwork of the 'Chansons de Geste' to which they listened in the market-places, handed down from age to age by the 'Cantori de Piazza.'

From these legends, both out of Celtic learning, came the matrix for Dante, Petrarch, and Boccaccio, Italian writers who worked from these legends to make a language for the new ideas of the Renaissance.

It was in Italy that the flame of the Renaissance was to ignite and grow to a brilliant light. The cities were the candle stands. Italy, after the "Donation of Pepin" was consigned to remain a collection of independent, but rival, states. Because the Italian states were small and the cities in those states were, by comparison, great, the cities had enormous influence.

Cities require services to live. They require community efforts for common needs. They reorganize the people by trade or calling, and they create new wealth in persons outside the established order of king, church, and baron. They force both state and church to loose their grip upon the city dweller. The city dweller seeks, and requires, knowledge.

The Influence of Gunpowder
and the Black Death

Add the influence of gunpowder, and the forces of change were irresistible. Before the Crusaders brought back knowledge of gunpowder, the only outlet for a brilliant mind was in a church or the military. Armies were raised by calling peasants under their feudal obligations and, as each soldier brought his own clothes and weapons, the only matter of supply was food.

Gunpowder changed all of that. Armies had to be organized on a regular basis and trained to use these new weapons, guns. Everyone was not qualified to be a soldier with a gun as each had been before with only a spear or spike. And guns meant a munitions industry, the various industries which grew from arms sales, and a new class of wealth among these gun makers. This new class of wealthy persons was not interested in keeping the old order of society. These industries created new openings for brilliant minds, and those minds accepted the challenge.

The Crusades and its companion, the Black Death, had already disheveled society by killing so many landholders that great tracts of land changed hands or became fallow. Labor costs skyrocketed. The new landowner was not necessarily committed to the old order. And those who were of the old order had to bend to these new conditions or lose their laborers, as those laborers could easily find other work. And finally, these new holders of wealth wanted the luxuries they had learned of from the East. Italy flourished as the first to answer this call for new things. Venice, as the trader, succeeded to all the traffic of the Arabs and grew rich.

The Glories of Florence

But it was in Florence where the torch burned the brightest. Many of its citizens became unimaginably wealthy from its trade and manufacturing. They obtained wool from England and Europe and wove it into the fabulous cloth the crusaders had seen and then had described upon their return. Its silks, with the silkworm transplanted to the Po valley, were equal to any in the world. The Florentine merchant princes collected art and promoted learning of the classics. Fortuitously at the same time, the Turks were assaulting the gates of Byzantium, and the scholars of that city's university were able to flee to Florence before their city fell.

Cosimo de Medici (1389-1464) used his worldwide connections to accumulate books of the ancients and have them translated. Indeed, collecting books became a pursuit of the educated. Sarzana, a monk of the Roman church in Florence, resorted to any device to accumulate manuscripts, each of which had to be copied by hand. When he was elected Pope Nicholas V, his collection followed him to Rome to become the beginnings of the Vatican library. Upon his death this library contained 5000 volumes.

As though that were not bounty enough, a group of Germans was working at their benches to develop a **printing press** with movable type. They did it! With the printing press, copies of books collected in Florence and throughout the Italian peninsula became plentiful and were distributed throughout Europe. To make this discovery more remarkable, if the printing press had been invented a few years earlier, there would have been nothing to print and it might have been regarded simply as a curiosity. Had it been developed a few years later, there would have been much less to print as the Turks were destroying everything which fell into their hands.

The Council of Florence, 1439

The East had long been in a state of gradual decay, and a schism between the Eastern and Western churches had existed at least since 1054, but the Eastern emperor saw union of the churches as a way to defend Byzantium against the Mohammedan invasion then threatening his city. A council of union was held in Florence in 1439. A decree resolving the schism was duly entered though it was of little significance as Byzantium fell to the Turks four years later. But this council's unintended result was enormous. Greek scholars fertilized western minds.

Most of the Byzantine delegates, dressed in robes and beards of the East, were of shallow intellect, and the Florentines were put out with them to the point that Cardinal Bessarion had to struggle to keep the Italians in attendance. But there was one delegate who cared little for the Eastern church and less for the Western church: **Gemistos Plethon**. He had little interest in these deliberations designed for the self-perpetuation and promotion of clergymen. But outside of the council meetings he was a godsend. The Florentines had already had tantalizing tastes of Greek knowledge and were eager for more. They had heard of Plato but knew no more than the name. They were anxious to learn, and Plethon was anxious to teach.

Plethon's prodigious memory, in tones eloquent or grave, poured out knowledge of the ancient Greeks, and the listeners literally bathed themselves in his words. He answered their questions. When he left, their eagerness and their attention convinced him that he had planted an orchard. **Cosimo de Medici** was so impressed by Plethon that he opened the famous Florentine Academy and appointed **Marsilio Ficino** both teacher and translator. Ficino and his pupil **Pico della Mirandola** spread Grecian knowledge throughout Italy. Their students, **Johann Reuchlin** and **Melanchton** spread it over Germany.

For Europe, this was the beginning of the return of philosophy and the re-birth of **humanism**. The word "humanism" meant the awareness of the vital perception of the dignity of man and the glory of being a rational animal rather than living a mere "mining camp" existence. It is in that sense the word is used here. Recently the word has been used in a phrase "secular humanism" to mean a secular existence without a religious conscience, which is quite a different thing, and not within the contemplation of this work. It was the unbinding of the straight jacket of scholasticism to release the human spirit.

But this freedom did not come without a struggle. In *A History of Classical Scholarship* Sandys indicates, **"Scholasticism** may be described as a reproduction of ancient philosophy under the control of ecclesiastical doctrine." As we saw earlier from Augustine's *City of God,* the dogma developed that reason was simply a device to confirm church truths. This, with scholasticism as its vehicle, was the fixed principle of western Christianity outside the Celtic church.

With the beginning rays of the Renaissance, the Roman church was hostile to the return of Greek philosophy. Aristotle had said that reality was to be found in real objects by the use of one's senses of touch, taste, smell, sight, and sound, through a well developed plan for science. Suddenly, people were drawing conclusions contrary to church doctrine. To make it worse, the study of nature and earthly matters in this new light directed one's mind away from spiritual concerns. This practice was, of course, contrary to that church's position. The Roman church had an attachment to Aristotle from its earliest days which continued through the period of scholasticism, but it was only to Aristotelian method, not the content of his ethical or metaphysical ideas. An early example of such intolerance to the diffusion of learning was by Pope Gregory I (c. 540-604) who was very upset that one of his bishops taught a friend grammar.

The Roman church's solution to the invasion of these new ideas was to codify the ancient philosophy as if it were a law code and then reconcile it to church truths. This task was the work of **Thomas of Aquinas.** He reconciled the returned Grecian knowledge with that of his church's predefined Christian dogma by saying there were two sources of knowledge: theology and philosophy. Theology starts with God and descends downward towards man, whereas philosophy starts with things perceived and goes up to God; hence, there was no conflict between them. The church was then able to adopt Aristotle's writings "lock, stock, and barrel" as dogma. Aquinas made Aristotle an ally by subverting his work. Its outer bounds were defined.

That church's position was enlarged: the writings of Aristotle were accepted as irrefutable truth. These writings became a part of church doctrine. Thus, if a new finding or observation conflicted with a statement of Aristotle, that church considered itself to be the arbiter between the contestants, just as it had been in matters of faith. Remember our ball with the light inside? The church simply added a few more holes and rubbed places on its surface. Nevertheless, the light was still confined and managed. When **Galileo** came to conclusions about the heavens contrary to the writings of Aristotle, he was imprisoned because he would not accept the decision of church authority holding him to be incorrect.

But there was no turning back. In 1350, virtually no one in Europe could read Greek. By 1500, thousands of people were studying it every day. That **Botticelli** could paint a nude and give it a pagan deity's name was unthinkable in 1350, but he did it 100 years later.

Humanism and Its Influence

What is this humanism that so changed people's lives and crept into every corner of our being? In the medieval period, life was regarded as a way station, a period of strife wherein a person, through clerical intercession, sought eternal salvation; earthly life was a penitence for eternal life. Sickness, poverty, and calamity were signs of God's wrath to be accepted and endured as indications of heavenly reward.

Humanism is the feeling that one has a life for its own sake. One must live vigorously, productively, and for beauty. Nature was no longer something that was simply there, but it was to be used, improved, developed, or simply appreciated. It was acceptable, and might be correct, to divert the course of a river. Good government was a virtue. People, at least philosophically, were suddenly free of a rigid hierarchy imposing the single requirement of serving God and earning salvation. They could have a passion for learning, be masters of arts and science, lovers of life, and seekers of beauty. There could be a Leonardo da Vinci. A person could have a direct relationship with God without a priestly hierarchy as the conduit between the two. Humanism was the vehicle by which Christianity would recapture its mystery, the individual's capacity to intuitively know God. It was a strong mechanism to force Christianity to lose its paganism.

The Renaissance and Reformation

To see how this knowledge was to flow across Europe we need to draw an imaginary line below England, through Belgium, then southeasterly to the northern tip of the Adriatic Sea, thence north to the mouth of the Oder River where it flows into the Baltic Sea. East of the line from the Adriatic to the Baltic, there is little of concern to our quest.

In the area west of that Baltic-Adriatic line, we find the drama of the Renaissance and its Teutonic counterpart, the Reformation, both of which so mightily influenced the English soul. How these forces of change and upheaval, this new knowledge with its humanism, affected those living to the north and the south of that Belgium-Adriatic diagonal was vastly different. It is those changes which are of most concern to us. South of that line, those who were its natives, were indelibly stamped **Romantic** by the Roman church. Those to the north of that line are essentially **Germanic**.

Both knowledge and humanism were in opposition to the old orders, whether religious or secular. Humanism holds that an individual can affect his own life, and he can intuitively know God. Such beliefs weaken the church since they say to the individual that he has control over his own destiny, and does not need a cleric to intercede for him. Knowledge makes people aware they can affect and shape their own lives, and gives each individual the ability to do so. Equally, if a person can determine one's own place, there is no need to subvert one's self through feudal tenure. The cities were becoming places of escape by rewarding the ordinary person for just such independent thoughts. Such notions strike at the very heart of feudalism and clerical absolutism.

The Roman church, through Thomas of Aquinas, was able to reconcile this new knowledge with existing theology. South of our diagonal, the church diverted the energy of the Renaissance into self-indulgence so that the fabric of society was not torn. The persons south of the diagonal used their newly won opportunities in beautiful clothes, houses, furniture, and art. The church cultivated a taste for art, and became a prime patron and sponsor of art. Church buildings were the works of the finest artists, such as Brunelleschi and Ghiberti. Then those churches were filled with the works of Giotto, Uccello, and Masaccio. But the organization of society was preserved with only a creeping change which could be controlled and directed by the sovran, the bishop, and the baron, none of whom wanted rampant change. They worked in concert to prevent it.

The people living to the north of that diagonal had always resented control, whether church or secular. It was their heritage that they honored a leader only so long as he was winning, or until the campaign was over. There was no single Germany for a pope, or anyone else, to seize. Were another to gain a victory over a German leader, it was often times meaningless, and the victor had won no more than a rope of sand. North of our diagonal, the Renaissance became the Reformation.

North of our diagonal, the impact of the Renaissance and the Reformation was in the field of education. And its effect was felt in humanism. Beginning with the reign of the Holy Roman Emperor, Otto I, and continuing until Bismarck, that vast middle expanse of Europe was never a state, though it pretended to be gathered under a German umbrella. It was a collection of principalities and dukedoms – all the offspring of feudalism – with only a language in common. They were in constant competition. Each had its own university, and one of those universities was always available for a dissident. Each of these universities had its own body of thought about humanism and other disciplines; consequently, the expansion of concepts regarding the role of an individual occurred north of our diagonal. France, by comparison, had only the University of Paris. In Paris, change could be guided; in the German universities, it was an explosion.

If there were ever a single voice of Northern Europe, it was that of **Erasmus** (1466-1536). Dutch by birth, but by acclamation a citizen of northern Europe and England, he learned Greek, translated the Bible from ancient sources, and proved the Roman church's Vulgate Bible was filled with errors. The effect was dynamic. Erasmus blended the wisdom of ancient Greece and Rome with the piety of Christianity. He made this mix of antiquity and Christianity into a new, regenerative force. Christianity again became a mystical, an intuitive, religion.

Couple Erasmus with the rambunctious **Martin Luther** (1483-1546), both operating within the very church itself, and the result is a ferocious combination for change. Luther spoke to the masses and to the ignorant, while Erasmus addressed the educated. Luther could have existed only in a Germanic region, as he was turbulent and unremitting. He fell from grace in one principality, and there was another to receive him. Each with his own appeal, these two men led growing armies to humanism.

The difference between the peoples north and south of our diagonal is illustrated by their art. The great flowering of artistic talent in the north, as among the Flemish, was overwhelmingly presented in pictures of landscapes, the sea, people, and their homes. Religious subjects were not sought after as they had been in the Romantic regions south of our diagonal. Rubens, van Dyck, Frans Hals, and Rembrandt, artists equal to any, won an unshakable place in the records of man's better footsteps, and were the inspiration for the English painter.

Protestantism sprang from this religious turmoil to the north of our diagonal. This word "protestant" has two distinct meanings. At first it was simply anti-papal, anti-ultramontane, meaning "against the pope over the mountains." Except for the short interruption of Cromwell, it was in this form, blended with mysticism, that Christianity assumed its place in England. This form accepted apostolic succession, the creeds, and the catholicity of Christianity. Apostolic succession is the belief that Christ appointed his disciples, the Apostles, and those, in turn, appointed bishops. Each succeeding bishop is consecrated by the hand of a predecessor reaching back to the touch of the Apostle and, through him, to Christ. In this form, by throwing off the pope, the adherents threw off any one person or instrumentality as a supreme control. A cleric might have interpretive skills, but he was not the gatekeeper to heaven, as, intuitively, each person might know God.

The second form of Protestantism rejected notions of a common creed and apostolic succession, in addition to the papacy. In the second group, each adherent claimed to himself the ability to seek and know the religious tenets without the intervention of clergy, whose sole function is to teach. While the Latin church had autocratic, rigid pronouncements and set forms, the French often ignored church restrictive mandates as they have been educated beyond its limits. Italy was always on a different footing: It had prosperity, freedom from feudalism, and commercial princes in an unstable confederation of states. Equally, the ardor of some of the adherents of Protestantism sometimes made them as intolerant as did the strictures of the Roman church. Sweden, an early Protestant state, adopted a law that if one left his church, he would be banished and not permitted to inherit property. Knowledge must be equal to religion, else the religion can be autocratic and narrow. These new ways of being a Christian turned Europe into a battlefield called the **Counter Reformation**. The Roman church tried by force to be all that it had been before these new ideas were introduced. That church was strong enough to snuff out the Renaissance in Italy and to slow its course in the north. It has been suggested by some that the Counter Reformation made the Roman church "simply another Protestant church" as it no longer accepted a baptism unless done by one of its own, whereas before that time anyone baptized as a Christian was accepted as a member of the Roman church.

Discovery of America Changed the World

As this knowledge and this humanism were flowing across the Alps, America was discovered. The world is round! The Mediterranean became a lake. Of this discovery Symonds wrote in *Renaissance*,

> [N]othing [was] so pregnant of results as this exploration of the globe. To say that it displaced the centre of gravity in politics and commerce, substituting the ocean for the Mediterranean, dethroning Italy from her seat of central importance in traffic, depressing the eastern and elevating the western powers of Europe,

opening the path of Anglo-Saxon expansiveness, forcing philosophers and statesmen to regard the Occidental nations as a single group in counterpoise to other groups of nations, the European community as one unit correlated to other units of humanity upon this planet, is truth enough to vindicate the vast significance of these discoveries. The Renaissance, far from being the re-birth of antiquity with its civilization confined to the Mediterranean, with its Hercules' Pillars beyond which lay Cimmerian darkness, was thus effectively the entrance upon a quite incalculably wider stage of life, on which mankind at large has since enacted one great drama.

We are ready now to turn to the English and their development from these nutrients of western civilization. All of them will play a part: Greek light, scattered by the Macedonians, made more luminous by the Roman mirror, brought to English soil by Roman citizens, and then tragically defused by the fall of Rome and the plan of the Afro-Latin church. The Arabs, though with one foot stamping out embers, were the ones to gather smoldering fires of ancient knowledge, stoke them to a new brightness, and hand them back to the West. The Italians grew bright flowers of art and literature as examples to us all. Northern Europe threw off the shackles of religious oppression. In this turmoil America was discovered, and instantly the Mediterranean sea was no longer the center of the world.

The inspiring force for this growth was a tribal religion which developed an ethical base, and was then infused with substance from the Greeks. But this religion, in lockstep with the West, was to be suppressed until both were freed by the second glow of the Grecian light.

The springboard of this renewal was friction and discord: the friction of the Crusades and the Black Death, each of such enormous tragedy that their sheer magnitude wore thin the shackles on the ankles of the Westerner. The friction of gunpowder and the printing press, the first to release men for new endeavors, and the second to give them access to knowledge to direct those endeavors. The discord was the renewal of classical knowledge.

Of course the elements are mixed differently in England. Otherwise, the English would be like Europeans. Now we shall try to find how these elements were blended to make the English the English.

Book Two

The English

Whence the English Came

7 THE BIRTH OF ENGLAND

England's geography and its settlement
by Germanic tribes with a glimpse of
their character and organization.

Gildas of Bath, who lived from c. 516-570, used these words
to describe this island home of our quarry.

> The island of Britain, situated on almost the utmost
> border of the earth, towards the south and west, and
> poised in the divine balance, as it is said, which supports
> the world, stretches out from the south-west towards
> the north pole, and is eight hundred miles long and
> two hundred broad, except where the headlands of
> sundry promontories stretch further into the sea. It is
> surrounded by the ocean, which forms winding bays,
> and is strongly defended by this ample, and, if I may
> so call it, impassable barrier, save on the south side,
> where the narrow sea affords a passage to Belgic Gaul.
> It is enriched by the mouths of two noble rivers, the
> Thames and the Severn, as it were two arms, by which
> foreign luxuries were of old imported, and by other
> streams of less importance.

This island is like a slightly upturned dish with the high rim
raised against the north Atlantic winds and rains to deflect their
violence before they reach the rolling plains of central and eastern
England. It is an ideal agricultural area, laced with rivers and rich in
arable lands as well as useful ore. To those willing to work, it can yield

a rich harvest. The Phoenicians had sailed to Britain for tin. The Celts, before the Romans, had a brisk trade, measured with coins, with their Gallic cousins living in present-day France.

The England of today, the one whose character and capacity we seek, began with the Angles, the Saxons and the Jutes, three Germanic tribes who replaced the Romans and displaced the Celts. The Romans left in A.D. 410; then the Germans, unnourished by the fruits of Mediterranean cultures, initially came in small waves, perhaps by invitation, then in increasing numbers as they realized they had come to "a more opulent country...under a more genial sun" than that which they had left. Displace the Britons, they surely did, as the Celts were pushed to present-day Wales and Cornwall, or back to the continent where they established a new homeland, Brittany. While there are scant records of the Germans bringing their women, nothing suggests any early influence of the Celts upon the Germans. These three pagan Germanic groups, the Angles, the Saxons and the Jutes, virtually cleared present-day England of other influences. They brought their own system of law and of government, both of which were entirely new to the area.

These German tribesmen were hunters who had been pushed from the East by the Huns. Their organization was tribal, and they were without a fixed attachment to place as the Romans had been. Their possessions were those items they could carry easily in their travels about their hunting grounds.

A Comparison of Roman and Germanic Law

These people had brought with them a system of law based entirely on the person: it was personal. Their law looked to the individual and that person's oath. This idea was entirely different from the Roman law and its Justinian code enforced on the continent. Rome had begun with the city itself, and it conquered its neighbor, and this new area became part of Rome. Rome never skipped over territories for distant prizes. It always grew in an orderly fashion. Rome required a law that protected the state and accommodated the new citizens. It spoke first of the state, the land, the territory. This distinction continues to this day and has colored each step taken by the inhabitants of this island called England. In Italy, as an example, through need, every home was a fortress. In England, by law, every home was a castle. The legal rampart of the castle was always more effective against the siege of a king than were the walls of the fortress. On the continent, law was what a legislature declared it to be. In England, law is what is decided by the courts on a case-by-case method, the "common law."

Indelible marks of the Germans were made, too, on the shape of the English government: each tribe had a **witan**, an assembly of noblemen, who met to determine the laws of the tribe and to elect one of their number as chief, later to be regarded as a king. The person chosen to serve as leader, whether called chief or king, did so at the witan's pleasure, and the witan did, on occasion, strip their king of authority and elect another in his place. Or, the witan might pass over the next male heir and select another member of the family. When the group went into battle, the witan would choose the one to lead them, and that leader could be a person other than the king. Should that leader lose to the enemy, or make an unfavorable treaty at the end of battle, the tribe would simply ignore what that person did. Real power, then, was vested in the witan, a body which ultimately evolved into a parliament.

Local self-government was through groups called "hundreds" or "folk moots," and its laws were administered by elected magistrates. These folk moots had authority to tax, and to collect tithes. It was this authority which gave the commoners entry into government, and ultimately led to the creation of a House of Commons. At first they might meet upon a village green, or common, and anyone could attend to shout their approval or dissent. While there were many more steps to be taken to create a parliamentary body, this early seizure of taxing authority was the key to opening doors along the way.

The Role of Women

The Germans' great sense of personal independence, compatible with social order, allowed them to develop their personal legal system. They differed from any other group in their belief in personal freedom and their attitude toward women. This might be compared with the Latino-Italianate attitude as later demonstrated in Verdi's *Il Trovatore* where the mother is revered but the lover is cast aside. In *Researches into the Natural History of Mankind*, Pritchard, the ethnologist, wrote that alone

> among the barbarous nations [the Germans] were equally distinguished for the cleanliness of their habits and for the comparative purity of their morals. In two remarkable traits the Germans differed from the Sarmatic, as well as from the Slavic nations, and indeed from all those other races to whom the Greeks and Romans gave the designation of barbarians. I allude to their personal freedom, and regard for the rights of men; secondly, to the respect paid by them to the female sex, and the chastity for which the latter were celebrated among the people of the north. These were the foundations of that probity of character and self-respect and purity of manners, which may be traced among the Germans and Goths even during pagan times, and which, when their sentiments were

60

enlightened by Christianity, brought out those splendid traits of character which distinguish the age of chivalry and romance.

Arnold's *Lectures on Modern History* sharply points out that "we, this great English nation, whose race and language are now overrunning the earth, from one end of it to the other," would never have been without this Germanic presence.

That the Germans "were not nourished by the fruits of Mediterranean cultures" and the English were inheritors of those qualities recited by Pritchard is largely due to the German defeat of the Romans in A.D. 9 under **Herman**, whose Latin name was Arminius. Herman had served in the Roman army and knew of its cruelties and oppression. When he returned to his homeland after such service, he saw the oppression the Romans were inflicting upon his own people. He determined he would free them, so he quietly recruited his own and neighboring tribes to fight for their own liberation. Ultimately he organized a sufficient band, and, by guerilla warfare, he defeated the Romans in Teutoberg Woods near Detmold. While the Romans returned to avenge this defeat, they never again mounted a true offensive against these Germanic peoples.

The Germans on English Soil

The lushness of the English countryside tied these Germanic peoples to the ground. Each family was given a strip of land for planting, and after the harvest, everyone's cattle ran on common pastures. There was very little need to travel as one town was much like another. Only military service took one from home, but even then, such service had to be limited so that crops could be planted and harvested. When we recall we are concerned with a people who loved to fight and who were fierce, independent folk, and ones who accepted a leader in battle only if he were successful, we can see the magnitude of the change taking place. They were sturdy people who were beginning to direct their energies more to the ground and less to combat. But these sturdy people retained their individual sense of freedom, surrendering neither to the demands of constant warfare, nor to a never-ending struggle for mere existence.

The Saxons had settled in the south of England, while the Angles began primarily in the east. In the north the smaller tribes were swallowed up by what was to become Northumbria. Middle England became Mercia. In the seventh century Mercia got the upper hand over Northumbria. In 825 **Egbert** of Wessex, West Saxons, defeated Kent. Egbert defeated Mercia in 829 and, with that victory, he was the first to be called "King of the English." Through that victory, he acquired sovereignty over the river Thames, England's highway to the advantages of the world.

8 THE CELTIC CHURCH AND CHRISTIANITY

The earlier arrival of Hellenic Christianity with the
Romans, its preservation by the Welsh and Irish,
and its influence through the time of the Danes.

Christianity came to Ancient Britain as a traveling companion
to the army and merchants of Rome. It spread incredibly well in Britain
and, by the fourth century of the Christian era, it was as well organized
as that in Gaul or Spain. In A.D. 314 the British church sent three
bishops to a church council at Arles. Three bishops also attended a
council in Rimini in A.D. 360.

Because the Roman empire was being drained by the struggles
along its northern frontier, its army was withdrawn from Britain in A.D.
410, but this withdrawal did not slow the growth of the Celtic church.
In *Nennius*, Morris says that **Arthur**, of legendary fame, "carried the
Cross of our Lord Jesus Christ for three days and nights" in the battle
of Mount Baden, c. 410, and "carried the image of the holy Mary, the
everlasting virgin.." in the battle of Guinnion fort. Beginning about 430,
the Briton Patrick was a missionary of the Celtic church to the Irish.
About A.D. 400 **Pelagius**, a scholarly British monk, arrived in Rome
and reviled the church in that city for its self-indulgent worldliness.
The things he saw led him to question the need for a church. The
church in Rome condemned him for these expressions, and declared
him to be a heretic. In the minds of many, however, Pelagianism was
an expression of the self-reliance of the English, and has remained, in
their opinion, a hallmark of English character.

Fastidius (fl. 420-430) wrote *On the Christian Life*, a work
completely devoid of fanaticism. His study is consistent with other

writings of Celtic Christians, as nowhere in the annals of the Celtic church is there the slightest hint or thought suggestive of a capacity for persecution. The clerics of the Celtic church were noted for their humility and unworldliness, and for their voracious appetite for knowledge.

Celts Preserved Hellenic Christianity During the Dark Ages

The arriving Germanic tribes gradually pushed the British, or Celtic, people, with their church, westward to Cornwall and Wales. This church, practicing a meek, unworldly Christianity, quickly lost contact with churches on the continent. In a few years, when the church again made its appearance, it blossomed into the seat of knowledge in the west.

The Celts kept the light of Greek knowledge which was woven into the Christianity they had received from the shores of the Mediterranean. Sadly the remainder of the west, however, was rapidly putting out the Grecian light and wrapping itself in almost total darkness.

By A.D. 500 a teaching monastery was practicing at **Aranmore** and by c. 520 a monastery was opened at **Clonard** which, under the Welsh, kept 3000 students at all times. Until the Celts opened other schools, Clonard may have been the only source of Grecian knowledge in the western world. It was assumed that if one knew Greek, that person was from Ireland. **Aldheim** (650-709) was educated under the Irish scholar **Maidulf**, the founder of a monastery at **Malmesbury**. He mastered the Greek idiom as though he were a native. Aldhelm has been called the father of Anglo-Latin verse.

The missionaries of the Celtic church were persevering and far-reaching. They went first to the Picts and the Scots and made a private lake of the Irish Sea. They moved among the Germans, especially those in Northumbria. At **Lindisfarne**, they established a monastery and school which flourished until it was sacked by the Danes in the ninth century.

The abbey at **Clonmacnoise** was founded in 541. **Alcuin**, of Charlemagne's court and one of the few intellectuals on the European continent outside Byzantium, was educated by Colcu of this abbey. The Celts preserved for Christianity the notion that an individual has worth and importance. The Celtic church, unlike its Afro-Latin counterpart, remained Neo-Platonistic. It fostered knowledge and independence of thought, an influence which stood quite apart from the numbing brine of ignorance, and later scholasticism, fostered by the Roman church.

The students of the Celtic church in Ireland, with outposts in northern England, were the founders of those libraries which did exist in Europe. The missionaries of the Celtic church were in almost total control of northern Europe to the exclusion of the Roman church. In their zeal to learn, these Celtic missionaries absorbed Latin and adopted the organization of the Roman church, perhaps an invitation to their own demise.

While establishing libraries, members of the Celtic church were the authors of the tradition of education in the western world, a concern abdicated by the Roman empire. **Columba** (521-597) a student at Clonard and one of its missionaries, opened a teaching monastery at Iona in the Hebrides. His followers preached across Europe and down into Italy, with **Dungal** going as far south as Modena where he died in 826. All the way from Ireland to Modena, these persons organized libraries and set up schools.

In contrast, the Roman church, from its earliest beginnings in Africa, was without a tradition of Greek knowledge or devotion to education. **Tertullian** was suspicious of general education and would forbid it. **Augustine of Hippo** would tolerate schooling as long as it was kept subservient to the Roman church. **Gregory**, an educated man regarded as one of the fathers of the medieval church, suppressed all classical Latin writings except those of Virgil. He regarded such light or frivolous writings as inconsistent with the study of Scripture. It was Gregory who insisted upon the use of Vulgate Latin and the Vulgate Bible, a Bible which reached back to the Hebrew text and erased the Greek influence with its teaching of humanism.

Rome itself had long before lost its bilingual education; furthermore, Roman schools became increasingly pedantic and superficial as the imperial government became more autocratic. The attitudes of the clerics of the Afro-Roman church towards education were in conflict with the Greek fathers, such as **Clement** and **Origen**, who regarded a liberal culture as indispensable to Christianity. So it was that the Celtic church was indispensable in establishing the basis for education north of the Alps and for its revival to the south of the Alps until Frederick II, Holy Roman Emperor, showed an interest which the Roman church was unable to suppress.

The brightest blooms in England, and indeed of the West, were of the Celtic tradition and included, in addition to the few we have named, **Alcuin**, the poet **Caedmon**, the Venerable **Bede**, and **John Scotus Erigena**, (810-877). Alcuin was the intellectual father of the Carolingian Renaissance. Caedmon, a monk of the Celtic monastery at Whitby, is regarded as the father of Anglo-Saxon verse. Bede was a cleric who aligned himself firmly with the Roman church though he had been trained in the Celtic tradition and, through that, had a knowledge of Greek. He did speak warmly of the piety and unworldliness of Celtic clerics, but he was strong in his opposition to that church as an organization. Bede is referred to by some as the father of English history, yet he never mentioned Patrick or Arthur, both of

66

whom must have been known to him, judging from the great number of sources mentioned in the introduction to his *Historica Eccestiastica*. John the Scot, Erigena ("Erigena" may mean "Irish born"), so unlike those of the Roman church, knew Greek, was familiar with the Neo-Platonistic writers and Aristotle, and accepted reason as being of primary importance.

As we have seen, Christianity entered England through Celtic missionaries, but Pope Gregory did not know this when he sent **Augustine of Canterbury** to Christianize the English. Bede tells us in *A History of the English Church and People* that when Augustine arrived in 597, he learned that Christianity was already present in England, and he wrote Gregory that, though Christianity existed on the island, he regarded some of the practices as peculiar. Gregory's answer was to accept as much as was proper, make only the changes which were needful, and be only as disruptive of existing practices as was absolutely necessary. Augustine, neither strong nor possessed of initiative, followed those instructions slavishly. Where he did make changes, Augustine adapted them from the Gallican church rather than the liturgy of the Romans. Because the ancient Gallican church was the basis of Celtic practices, the changes were insignificant. Those forms continue as the basis of the Anglican service to this day. While Augustine has been called the apostle to Kent, **Aidan**, of the Celtic church, is known as the apostle to England.

The Celtic and Roman churches had developed real differences in styles and forms of worship, and these differences grew as the influence of the Roman church increased. How should they calculate the day upon which Easter fell? How does a cleric cut his hair, his tonsure? Not until 664 at the **Council of Whitby** could the conflicts between them be partially resolved. By that agreement, Rome took the upper hand. But, again, the changes made were not disruptive to the underlying fabric of Celtic religion. The primary effect was in church organization, and that was merely an overlay on the existing faith. The church in England continued to be Hellenic in content, albeit with a Roman organization. These differences were maintained, at least in part, by England's physical separation from the continent, a separation that fostered a people increasingly unlike their continental neighbors. After the arrival of Augustine, each of these two churches, Celtic and Roman, had their separate periods of ascendancy. The king of Northumbria, and his subjects, were converted to the Roman sect in 627. That king's grandson did not follow his grandfather, but instead, he joined the Celtic church. **Egbert**, crowned about 830 as the first king of the English, had been raised in the court of Charlemagne. Since France had abandoned the Gallic service in favor of the Roman liturgy, Egbert must have been familiar with both forms. Egbert established schools in his court on the Alcuin's Carolingian model, and his schools were open to noblemen as well as clerics and royalty.

Egbert's grandson, **Alfred the Great** (849-899), who may well be the most intellectual of English monarchs, was reared in the country of the Celtic church and studied under the Welshman Asser. His older brother, Aethelstan, was a great collector of books, works of art, and religious relics. Undoubtedly these accomplishments influenced Alfred, who after two trips to Rome and after reaching maturity, learned to read and write both the Latin and Saxon languages. He had his companion, Asser, record writings or sayings which pleased him; then he would translate these into Saxon and have them distributed throughout his realm.

Throughout his life, Alfred showed an affection for, and gave support to, the Celtic church. Undoubtedly the teachings of that church caused his lament that so few could understand a divine service. As a result, he collected the best of the religious writings and laws of all the earlier English kings and had them reduced to writing in the vernacular of the people so that they could be understood by his subjects.

Alfred established a school at his court for both nobles and clergy similar to that which Alcuin had organized in Charlemagne's court. He had parts of the Bible, Bede's *History of the English*, and other works translated into the contemporary language of his people. He was himself one of the translators of those works.

The Arrival of the Danes and Their Adoption of English Customs

The Danes had been plundering the English coast for almost a century, and Alfred was finally able to defeat them. Alfred made a peace with them which included a division of England between Alfred's Saxons and the Danes. As part of the peace agreement, the Danes adopted the Christian faith. The Danes, north of London, were in an area heavily influenced by the Celtic church. In 1013, the Danish royal line became sovrans of England. These Danes preserved the laws of Alfred's line and continued to use the written vernacular which Alfred had fostered.

On the continent, as the sterile water of ignorance seeped north, its flow was interrupted by the Englishman Alcuin in the Frankish court, and the seeds for a rebirth of knowledge were planted throughout the West by missionaries of the Celtic church traveling from Wales and Ireland. In England, the Celtic love of learning was not aggressively challenged, or perhaps it was ignored, until William I, but by then, its triumph was assured.

In these early days, we can identify a feeling of self-worth (lost to the others of the West until the Renaissance), a Celtic church-inspired love of learning which included a devotion to reason as made manifest by Erigena, and those qualities of the Germanic tribesmen as described by Pritchard, to indeed make the English "quite a race apart."

9 THE ENGLISH AND THEIR LANGUAGE

The English, alone of the European peoples,
preserved and used a native written language.

The English, unlike their European cousins, used their own language. The Kentish Law Code, written about A.D. 600, is the oldest surviving manuscript in Old English. Its existence points also to other, earlier written documents because it evidences a developed written style. Annual historical records, called *Easter Annuals*, were also written in the vernacular, forming the basis of the *Anglo-Saxon Chronicles*. Not only were these Chronicles written in English, but some of the source material was translated from the Latin.

Nennius (fl. 796) wrote a history of the Saxon kings and recorded the legends of King Arthur. His work was in Welsh and later translated to the Vulgate. Only Old English, of all the European tongues, was used for verse, both secular and religious. **Rhyme**, as we know it today, was a gift of the Celts. The best known early verse is *Beowolf*. A surviving copy dates from about A.D. 1000, but it was written at a much earlier date. This use of the people's language can only be explained as a result of the influence of the Celtic church, an influence sadly suppressed by the Roman church as it forged its way across Europe.

The six centuries ending with the eleventh have been justly called the Dark Ages, with the tenth being held in lowest esteem. The Danes had overrun England. The Normans defeated the French, bringing an end to the line of Charles the Bald and its enlightenment. The Hungarians occupied both sides of the Alps. Perhaps miraculously, the Celtic tradition continued with such writers as **Aelfric** (c. 955-1030) who composed a Latin-English dictionary and wrote his "Homilies" with a preface in the Saxon language.

10 THE INFLUENCE OF WARS

The scant impact of wars on the English
compared with continental Europeans, and
war's influence in molding English character.

We have mentioned that military service was the one force strong enough to make a person leave home. But this duty of military service in England was unlike that on the continent. With the single exception of William I and his reign of terror, all battles on English soil were small – small in the numbers of people fighting in them, small in battle sites, and small in the time they took. Also England's involvement in foreign wars was slight when compared to the states of Europe. As a result, the sovran was not constantly seeking revenues from, and at odds with, his people. This lack of constant warfare meant the sovran and the people could have regular exchanges. It meant the noble person could be friendly with the merchant or the tiller of the soil. When conflicts became irreconcilable, the commoners with the king, or the commoners with the nobility, could act together for their mutual advantage.

Reaching forward in time, but illustrative of the differences between the English and those in Europe, we can compare the English civil wars of the mid-seventeenth century and the contemporaneous Fronde in France: both started as political and social conflicts. In England, solutions were achieved with gains for the commoner and for the nobles. This rapport with the commoners, this opportunity for gradual change, is a substantial reason why England enjoys a monarchy today. But in France, the Fronde (1648-1653) began as an effort to restrict rule by royal will, and it included social changes for the commoner. Almost at its inception, the commoners' social aims were abandoned and the war became purely political between the king and Parliament of Paris. The commoner had no interest in the outcome of such a struggle. The French people had to wait for horrid anguish of their revolutions to seek redress from royal oppression.

And in England, the relative peace enjoyed by the people undermined the numbing influence of an autocratic religion. In Europe, the unceasing and constantly changing struggle between king and aristocrats, or the grinding rampages of mercenaries without a war (though often with the blessing of their church), compelled the notion of sanctuary as a safe haven for the ordinary person. Under this doctrine one could take refuge in a church, and if asylum were granted, such person was safe from the forces of the crown or the law. There was no need for such a protection in England and the absence of this need reduced the importance of any church as an intervener, a meddler, into one's daily life.

So it was until the landing of the Danes: the Germanic tribes merged to become English. The notion of fixed boundaries adapted from the Roman church had slipped into civil use. The seats of intellectual growth in **Lindisfarne** and **York** were flourishing under the care of the Celtic church. And singularly so in the west, the English had retained a tradition of a written, vernacular language. The English have preserved their witan, folk moots, and hundreds, but by physical boundaries rather than tribes, and by persons seeking a spring crop rather than hunting a wild animal.

11 THE NORMAN CONQUEST

The invasion of England by the Normans,
the impact of William's tyrannies, and his
reorganization of the state and church in England.

At the beginning of the ninth century, Europe began to feel the scourge of the Vikings, who rampaged from Constantinople to North America. These Germanic peoples lived in an area which was demanding of, and unforgiving to, human habitation. They wanted out. They wrested parts of France and England for themselves. While the Danes were overrunning the English in the north, they destroyed the abbeys at Lindisfarne and at York. The abbey of York probably housed the finest library in the west outside of Byzantium.

Alfred was able to subdue the Danes and, as a result, England was divided between his Wessex and the **Danelaw**. This division lasted for a century until another conflict erupted and the Danes became sovrans of England. **Svegn**, the second of the Danish line, sent his Danish army home and reasserted the English law as published in the vernacular. As these Danes shared a German stock with the English, they shared a number of common values about how society was organized and governed. Since Alfred's peace, the Danes had adopted Christianity, so they shared a common religion. Remarkably, these Danes were well on the march to becoming Englishmen by 1066, and during the intervening years between Alfred and Harold, the crown had agreeably alternated between the English and the Danish lines.

In 1066, the Norseman **William the Conqueror** was the last to successfully lead an expedition of foreign blood to English soil. William's Norman ancestors had come from Norway and had lived for about 100 years in a part of the Frankish lands they called "Normandy," a stay which had an enormous impact on their character.

Vikings were fighting machines. "Berserk" is a Norse word referring to their frenzied fighting style. The Normans in those few years on Frankish soil learned about feudalism, became Christians of the Roman church, and developed French ideas of civilization. The continental practice of "constant warfare" was made for them.

In Europe, boundaries were only lines on a map which rarely traced a geographic barrier or had a precise location. Armies were usually peopled by mercenaries. If these fighters-for-hire had no war to go to, they often plundered as a form of recreation, or as their only means of livelihood. Marauding bands were always foraying for loot. A group of persons of that ilk simply took what it wished and destroyed at will. Sanctuary by the church represented a real need because it was the only safe haven respected by more than one faction. The church thus became meaningful in the life of the ordinary person. But at the same time, leaders of the marauding bands gave a portion of their loot to the same church and received the blessing of its priests. This constant warfare, coupled with the duplicity of local clerics, was made more cruel and unforgiving by the vise-like hold of feudalism. When William came to England in 1066, he brought all the circumstances and conditions with him.

In 1066 William came, he conquered, and he was crowned. He ruled as a tyrant for twenty-one years. He burned and he pillaged. He imposed the French language on the English. He assigned the land to himself and to his Norman and French supporters. He changed the organization of the courts to "county" ones, of the local count, as in France. He changed the persons of the church and enforced direct accounting to himself. He ordered the **Doomsday Book** compiled so that he would know of every asset in his realm: every pig, every chicken, every cart, everything of value. He brought in feudalism as a developed institution and imposed it on the English. In effect, rather than displacing the occupants as the Anglo-Saxons had done, he overlaid a new group and gave to them all the assets of the prior occupants. He smothered the English under a thick Norman carpet. He did, geographically, make England one nation but at a horrible cost to that nation.

Yet the tug to be English, and not Norman or continental, was irresistible. William's youngest son, **Henry I**, was called the "Lion of Justice." He reestablished Anglo-Saxon laws, created king's courts as an alternative to local baronial (county) courts, appointed competent judges, and sent them on circuit to the people. This king's grandson, **Henry II**, strengthened the court system and introduced trial by jury. The measures of these two kings curbed the barons. Unfortunately, after the murder of Henry II's appointed archbishop of Canterbury, **Thomas Becket**, the sovrans had increasing problems with the Roman church. Until then, even during the bleakest days of oppression in England beginning with William, a small window had remained open so that the sunlight of intellectual inquiry, and the fresh air of self-worth would not be lost. After this murder, it was going to be harder to keep that window open.

The Role of the Roman Church

The Roman church had not yet established itself in England as it had on the continent. Since the Council of Whitby in 664, persons such as Wilfred of York and Bede had struggled to suppress the Celtic faith and replace it with the Roman church, but had never been able to do so. The Roman church had been too weak to make itself a religious baron in England.

William refused to give fealty to Gregory VII and his successors. He reminded Gregory that his predecessors had never done fealty to

Gregory's. William's refusal was remarkable since Gregory, before his election as pope, had actively supported William in his invasion of England. William and his heirs not only resisted papal interferences in English affairs but they forbade appeals to Rome. Not until after the murder of Becket was William's grandson, Henry II, required to compromise with the clerics of the Roman church. However, this compromise related only to that church's land holdings and its elections. That compromise was made in order to preserve Henry's position between the clerics in England and Rome.

Henry II's second son, **John**, has been condemned by many as the worst sovran to sit upon the English throne. His error-strewn reign was as much a disaster in religious matters as it was politically. Yet it inadvertently served as a blessing to the English in at least one arena.

John began his career in 1199 by incurring the enmity of the French king when he inherited his father's lands in Normandy. The French king said those living in England must declare whether they be French or English, and if English, they would not be permitted to hold title to French land. This restriction infuriated the barons. In time, however, these losses would bend the eyes of the heirs of the Conquest to England and to their neighbors at home.

As if that were not enough, the Roman pope appointed a person as archbishop of Canterbury of whom John did not approve. John fought the pope for seven years. England was put under an interdict so that no sacraments other then baptisms could be performed. Finally John was excommunicated, i.e., expelled, from the church. After four years, when he was surrounded by opponents, and under threat of a French invasion of England to depose him as king, he became painfully aware he had lost his struggle with the papacy. He was required to submit humbly to the Roman bishop as his spiritual lord. Before this event, the Roman and the English churches had been bedfellows; now they were married and Rome was the autocratic husband.

The barons also struck. They enlisted the aid of the English to subdue their king. The nobles, both English and Norman, joined at Runnymede and forced John to sign the **Magna Carta**. For the first time the English, the Normans, and the French acted as one. William's carpet had been rent. England was again to be one country of one people. John lost everything. As Matthew of Westminster recorded of him on his deathbed, "he cursed all his barons…and [was] deprived of all his treasures, and not retaining the smallest portion of land in peace, so that he was truly called Lackland."

12 WILLIAM'S DARK AGE

Feudalism, brought to England by William,
was devastating to the growth of knowledge.

Anglo-Norman England from William I's landing in 1066 until the end of the fifteenth century was harsh, autocratic, and desolate, relieved only by the actions of so few persons their names can be counted on one's fingers, and punctuated by a scant number of events which were of unintended, or unwanted, result. It was a time of a curious and unparalleled mixture of freedom and oppression, of stability and lawlessness. It was one long struggle for the English to keep their own character against the almost unbearable strength of European feudalism, personified in the barons in the service of William, perpetuated by their offspring, and augmented by the Roman church.

Feudal lords, jealous of their own possessions, kept France in bondage until the French revolution, and in Germany, the first breach of feudal rule was not until the conquests of Napoleon. Their kindred who came with William were determined to do the same to England. Fortunately, their grip never became so great as it was in either France or Germany.

Feudalism was an outgrowth of the ancient Germanic tribes. Each tribe was, as we saw earlier, a confederation, which, by oaths and loyalties, elected their leaders through assembly. As they were pressed into Europe by the Huns, they were compressed together, but still, each tribe had an enormous tract of land to which it was confined. Yet, each tribe had no system of administration or taxation, a necessary corollary of limitations of movement and self defense. Hence, areas were given over to individuals in return for military service. Each of these persons, called barons, in turn, assigned portions of his lands to others for a similar duty to that baron. Each baron established his own courts to collect fines and enforce laws. Most cities and towns were within a baron's land and, as a baron did not wish to promote trade, which undermined his authority, towns offered no place of growth or refuge. As a baron became secure, he would raid his neighbor's land. Anyone not in this hierarchy of feudal obligation either entered it by swearing service in return for land and protection, or had no protection and no redress: a serf at the mercy of all. Land, by law, was passed to a baron's first born male heir, and each person of a baron's family had to marry within his own station. This rule made society increasingly rigid and fixed.

In a feudal state, a "great council," the witan, was called by the king. And in such a state, the witan grew to include only barons. A meeting of the witan had to be called to declare war, to obtain money from the barons, or to punish a baron, as each of these required the consent of the barons. To curb or punish a baron, or to obtain money, the king was required to call a meeting of the council. At such meetings, while the barons had to acknowledge their feudal duty to the king, the barons would never agree to anything until their own grievances were settled. This system was aristocratic in the extreme. It was this feudalistic rigidity, with its banner of chivalry to display its inbred vanity, in lockstep with its gross cruelties (including instant death for offenses), which was brought to England by William.

Under feudalism, the barons and the king were at once hostile, yet joined. The baron recognized his duty to his sovran, but he would brook no interruption on his own lands, where he was sovran. These barons and the sovran constantly struggled among themselves over who had the ascendancy on the most petty of issues. A king wanted to go to war where he would lead his barons as his vassals. The barons resisted unless they saw plunder for themselves. The king wanted trade, which required some ties to the people; the barons wanted things to be as they were. At once, a hostility and a kinship existed, an antagonism and a pulling together. These forces threatened to stifle the life from England. They were merely interrupted, but not seriously abated, until the appearance of the Black Death.

Stubbs' *Constitutional History of England* informs us that "feudalism in both tenure and government was, in so far as it existed in England, brought full grown from France." England had not known of constant warfare, nor of estates of lands of such unmeasurable enormity as were those in France or Germany. Taken together they spawned such an oppression that any relief would be welcomed.

John added the last straw. John made worse the autocratic weight of oppression by his submission to the papacy. The clerics of the Roman church were as grasping and as invidious to the growth of society as were the barons. These clerics were armed with the ever ready pretense of claiming church duties should anyone complain of their actions.

Fortunately, however, before William's arrival in England, with the incursion of the Danes, England started to become increasingly rigid and aristocratic. This may have been a saving influence because it spawned confederations of freemen who bound themselves together for their mutual protection and companionship. The existence of these groups continued through William's Dark Age. For the next 300 years these groups, by almost imperceptible steps, struggled to carry a beacon of individual self-worth, and a night-light for a free mind.

13 RE-LIGHTING THE LAMP

The absence of both foreign wars and conflict
between feudal lords and the sovran, combined
to regenerate "Englishness" of the people and
to reassert the spirit of intellectual curiosity
nourished by Hellenistic knowledge which
had been kept for the English but denied
to those on the continent. Individualism
was made secure by the two tragedies of the
Black Death and the Hundred Years' War.

To the Norman William goes the credit of uniting England into a single state, though the people within that state were not united until the reign of John. These Normans, Norsemen, where kindred spirits of German stock, yet this kinship did not appear until the reign of **Henry I**, the Lion of Justice, who collected the English laws in their native tongue. This action was a slap at the barons as it resurrected a system of laws known to the people, but not always serving the interests of the barons. Henry I also created courts answerable to him rather than to a baron or to the church. These changes gave an opening for the ordinary Englishman to begin to look to the sovran and away from the baron.

Henry I ascended the throne in 1100. As Gildas had written some 600 years before, England was still "situated on almost the utmost border of the earth." This separation was as important to England after William's conquest as at any time in her history. England was rarely threatened with foreign invasion, hence the notions of "Englishness" had a chance to settle on these Norman and French foreigners. A part of this "Englishness" was that the sovran could accept local self rule and could tolerate a national parliament. Indeed, both ideas served the sovran's interests against those of the barons. When people are not fighting, they can talk. If they can talk to their king, they are not so confined as they would be if allowed to speak only to a feudal baron. This practice of popular communication increased so that the able **Edward I**, 1272-1307, frequently consulted with his subjects outside of any formal parliament.

Edward I has been called "The English Justinian." His reign was remarkable not only for its legislative activity, but also for its changes in the administration of justice. Of his reign, Blackstone said "that more was done in the first thirteen years of his reign to settle and establish distributive justice of the kingdom than in all the ages since that time put together." Of the title "English Justinian," Lord Campbell remarked, "Absurdly enough, as the Roman Emperor merely caused a compilation to be made of existing laws, whereas the object now was to correct abuses, to supply defects, and to remodel the administration of justice." Justinian's work was one of hindsight, while Edward's work looked to the future.

An instrument of immeasurable importance to self-rule in those wretched days was the town. Town charters were issued with increasing frequency by sovrans, and notably John, as a source of revenue outside the control of the barons. These independent, chartered cities were in the forefront of the struggle between baron and king. But, most important, cities were a weapon which worked to the advantage of the people by creating an oasis for independent thought and places of trade. Trade meant wealth outside the feudalistic order. Bias against the barons was also strengthened as many town charters had this provision: should one leave his lord to live in that town for the space of a year and not return to his lord, he became a free person. Towns were better than any church for sanctuary as they were work sites of independence rather than simply a place to hide.

After John's reign, the Roman church became more entrenched. As the holder of increasingly large estates, its influence was more widespread. It could be a feudal lord as treacherous as any baron. Happily these double yokes of ecclesiastic and secular feudalism were made bearable by the richness of the soil and by the wool trade, both of sufficient abundance to satisfy the lords and leave a goodly reward for their vassals.

Freedom from foreign intervention, the bounty of the farms, and the growth of free cities allowed England to strengthen the authority of the king, on the one hand, and to weaken the strangle hold of the barons and the church on the other. These changes in power meant less scrutiny from above and more freedom for the ordinary mortal.

The window to the mind was still open. In the twelfth century England produced the finest minds of western Christendom. The intellect, or what there was of it, of this entire medieval age, rests on Englishmen, such as Alcuin and **John Scotus Erigena**. Erigena was the first outside the early Celtic church since the Ancient thinkers, to fuse Christianity with Neo-Platonsim. A papal librarian who had learned Greek in Constantinople wondered how this "barbarian" living on the very edge of the world could comprehend the mysteries of Greek and impart them to another tongue. John the Scot knew the ancient writers and it was said his translations from the Greek were so fine as to themselves require an interpreter. His impact as a Neo-Platonist was such that Pope Honorius II, 1226, ordered some of his works be burned as heretical, a certain sign of success.

Also in the twelfth century, the Saxon **John of Salisbury** (1110-1180) was known for his utilitarian bent of mind. He was thought of as a humanist before its time. **Robert Grossteste** straddled the end of the century. As chancellor of Oxford, Grossteste was a reformer railing against the excesses of both the pope and the king. But his real contribution lay in that new arena of experimental scientific thought which opened the path for reason to break the shackles of clerical authority. His education rested on the liberal arts and literature, including Greek and Latin. Wycliffe believed Grossteste approached Aristotle in impact. Grossteste was one of the few persons to grasp the idea of unity of knowledge.

Grossteste pointed to **Roger Bacon** (1214-1292), who was one of the first to appreciate the work of the Arabian scholars, whose writings demonstrated the defects in the thought patterns of Bacon's continental contemporaries. This century was also the time of **William of Occam** 1285-1347) a Franciscan monk who taught at Oxford. He stated, as did the ancient Greeks, that individual things were the only ones to exist and each thing could be apprehended and recognized by the mind. William reasoned from real things to general principles (inductively) rather than from general principles to particular things (deductively).

Introduction to Deductive Reasoning

Deductive reasoning is a method of reasoning in direct opposition to that of the Roman church. As we saw earlier, Thomas of Aquinas had "reconciled" Greek learning with the doctrines of the Roman church by simply allowing more light to escape from inside the ball. Through this method of thought, the Roman church could "know" the source of light; hence, it could measure available knowledge. William of Occam, on the other hand, stated the things a person could know were those on the surface of the bass as they were illuminated from an outside source of light. William's reasoning is the hallmark to Jefferson's expression of "the illimitable freedom of the human mind."

The thirteenth century contained another reward: **Henry III** as sovran was too fond of both the French and the papacy. He wished to levy a heavy tax for the pope, but the barons refused, saying, "the minor gentry" would not contribute. The king then sent delegates to each shire to persuade them to do so. The shires continued to refuse. The local representatives met at Oxford to talk, to "parler," and one of their resolutions was for regular talks, parliaments, with the king. So it was that the witan which became the "great council," in turn, became a parliament, and was ultimately to meet on a fixed basis. The lubricant for this evolution was an acknowledgement that the authority to tax resided in the local community.

At the close of this century, Henry's son, Edward I, issued laws which curbed both the barons and the church in their insatiable greed for land and power. The crown jewel of his reign was a law that prevented the buyer of land from becoming the vassal of the seller. This law was the beginning of a legal assault on feudalism.

But that was not all: Edward I had laws enacted to aid merchants, provided for an army outside the control of the barons, made the hundreds and the shires responsible for criminals, and, as a strong king, ratified the Magna Carta. In 1295, he convoked the so-called "model parliament". The impact of his reign was so enormous that by 1322 the **Statute of York** was adopted. This statue required that all future laws had to be passed in Parliament by king and commons, a radically unthinkable idea. It was in these early days that the present form of government, king, lords and commons, was put into place. During all these days, independent cities, blossoming into new sources of wealth, were a catalyst for change.

The fourteenth century saw the strengthening of both houses of Parliament. Despite Edward I's careful education of his son in the art of statecraft, **Edward II** was incapable of learning and was, as Dr. Stubbs wrote, "the first king after the Conquest who was not a man of business." He was both frivolous and weak, allowing the barons to take the reins of government. Edward's effort to save England's claim to Scotland resulted in a bitter defeat by Robert Bruce. Defeat made him weaker in his struggles with the barons. Squabbles between the barons and with the king, each trying to curry favor with the people, caused the adopting of a rule that no statute was valid without the consent of Commons. Edward's wife was a party to these struggles too. In 1329, her meddling provoked the barons to violence. Edward II was imprisoned and forced to renounce the throne. Parliament quickly chose his son, Edward III, to replace him. Despite horrid treatment, designed to make Edward II ill and die, he remained fit. He was murdered that same year.

Edward III ruled for fifty eventful years. His claim to be king of France provoked the Hundred Years War. His reign saw the arrival of the **Black Death**, and he repudiated the concessions made to the pope by John. This Edward took the first steps to use lay administrators in government. He instituted the Order of the Garter, and his incessant need for money meant the frequent recalling of the Commons, and firming of its role. As an unintended legacy, his sons, John of Gaunt and Edmund of York, founded the rival houses of Lancaster and York.

John of Gaunt made alliances with **John Wycliffe** (1320-1384), a master of Balliol College. Wycliffe was the first to abandon Latin for clerical papers by the singular feat of writing in English. He translated the Bible into English. The enormity of such a thing is hard for us to conceive, but until his translation, the Bible, within the sweep of the Roman church, existed only in Vulgate Latin, a language known only to a very few clerics. A translation of the Bible ran counter to the deliberate plan by the Roman church to use the Bible as the cornerstone of its monopoly of knowledge. The church insisted that lay persons not be permitted to know its contents, but only those things they were told about its contents. However, it was not until the next century, when Erasmus made his translation of the Bible, that the western world became aware of the enormity of the errors in the Bible authorized by the Roman church.

All these forces of change for loosening the grip of oppressive power were magnified many times over and given an incalculable impetus by the Black Death, a "gift" from the Moslems during the Crusades. The Black Death cut its way through England in 1348 and 1349 and again in 1362 and 1369. Epidemics followed until the 1500's. The labor force was ravaged and contracted; arable land lay fallow, and wages skyrocketed. This labor shortage led to a conversion from farming to wool production because it required less labor. Wool production also brought increased trade, resulting in urban growth. As the cities prospered, both the church and the barons lost their holds on the people.

This century closed with giant leaps toward true parliamentary government. In 1399 Parliament declared the throne to be vacant and installed **Henry IV** as king. This vigorous Parliament, unimpeded by a king who feared he could be deposed, made reforms: No money would be supplied the king until all wrongs had been righted; the royal accounts were to be audited; certain types of legislation could be initiated only in the House of Commons; and the king could reject, but not change, laws enacted by the Commons. Enacted, though not enforced, the fullness of these changes had to be delayed until the still-too-strong barons annihilated themselves in that otherwise worthless butchery known as the War of the Roses.

The resumption of the Hundred Years War in the first half of the fifteenth century freed the English people. War, then as now, made prices rise. Merchants and tradesmen prospered. It brought back to life a class of people with a new vigor: freemen, yeomen. During the war these freemen learned they were just as necessary, and just as effective, as the baron. In the peace that followed, they were not inclined to accept feudal obligations or clerical oppression. These people came to regard themselves as "English" and not "of a manor," as subjects of the monarch, and not of a baron.

As the towns prospered, a new harmony developed between those in the cities and those of the land. In England, unlike the continent, towns lacked walls and were never fortresses. When a true parliament was later established, the local landowner regularly represented the city dweller. the landowner was able to make a sufficient reward from the land so that he had money to invest. He was not afraid to innovate with, or to invest in, city-bound enterprises. This general prosperity, joined with their background of personal freedom described by Pritchard, made the English a practical and private people, preferring one and two story houses rather than apartments. These individual homes are the breeding ground of manners. After all, it is self-evident that one cannot have privacy without according that same right to others.

This harmony between the landowner and the merchant, their sharing of investments, and representation of one another in parliament, in "commons," of common people, promoted cross fertilization of the populace. A growing practice of intermarriage between those of the landholding and merchant classes, with the consequent strengthening of each line, became the rule rather than the exception. It was this cross breeding which prompted Kipling to write in *The English Flag*, "And what should they know of England who only England knows."

Chaucer (1340-1400) was, in a real way, the coming together of all the forces that were loosed upon the English. He was the son of a London wine dealer, a layman, a man with royal friends, a diplomat, and a member of Parliament, a man who had risen from yeoman, freeman, to be a king's squire. He recast the language of the English from a crude elementary speech to one incorporating the grace of continental languages yet retaining the earthly wit and charm of his forebears. His vigorous simplicity of tongue has since characterized the English language. None of its writers except Dryden in some of his plays – now happily forgotten – used the exaggerated polish of the French. Chaucer's versification is the foundation stone, built upon Celtic bedrock, for all the English poetry which would flow to the furthermost reaches of the earth.

14 SPRINGTIME IN ENGLAND

The Tudor's reign marked the end of internal
conflict left as a remnant of feudalism and a release
from the strangle- hold of the church. It was the
beginning of a non-clerical governing class, a
flowering of literature, and global perspective.

Springtime came to England in 1485. The stage was set by a conflict between the houses of Lancaster and York, a conflict later known as the **War of the Roses**. It was a struggle over succession of the crown and one fought by mercenaries. The conflict was inconclusive until Henry Tudor defeated Richard III at Bosworth. The reconciliation began when the victor ascended the throne as Henry VII with the blessing of Parliament, but without mention of a hereditary right. Henry, a Lancastrian, married Elizabeth, a Yorkist, and though rumblings continued, the great divide between these two houses came to a close.

The light of a mind began to glow in a way it had not done since the fall of Rome. Copernicus opened the universe. Explorers went round the horn of Africa to lower their anchors in Asian ports. Columbus sailed across the Atlantic.

Much of what would follow was foretold in this reign of **Henry VII**. Columbus made overtures to the English crown for aid in his explorations. Thought Henry expressed an interest in Columbus' ideas and talks were begun, Isabella of Spain was first to conclude an arrangement; as a result, this expedition did not come to fruition as an English venture. Henry responded by commissioning **Sebastian Cabot** to go to the new world. As a reward, he obtained the rich fishing waters off Newfoundland and the Atlantic coast of North America, with adjacent lands to be settled in the next century. For a later voyage,

Henry commissioned the construction of the first English naval vessel. Prior to that time merchant vessels had been commandeered when needed for public purposes. Henry VII obtained favorable trading rights with Scandinavian countries, with much of the cargo carried in vessels flying the English flag. He also broke the Venetian monopoly for transport of Mediterranean shipping.

In 1491 **William Grocyn**, a fellow at New College, may have been the first to deliver Greek lectures at Oxford. **Thomas Linacre**, also at Oxford and one of the first scholars of the "new learning" of the Renaissance, translated the works of Galen and taught Greek to Erasmus and More. He was also physician to Henry VIII. **John Colet** studied Greek in the Florence of Lorenzo Medici, the Magnificent, but rather than view Greek simply as literary achievements, like the Italians, he was practical in his use of this new learning. He also disregarded all the medieval writers "as corruptions of the schoolmen." Though the idea of a break with the Roman papacy would never have occurred to him, his influence materially undermined medieval thought in favor of the new learning. He did, however, oppose the accepted practice of auricular confessions and of a celibate, unwed, priesthood. His simplicity found warm and useful places in the minds of both Thomas More and Erasmus, who so effectively spread Colet's theology.

Sir Thomas More, a student of Colet, Grocyn, and Linacre, and a friend of Erasmus and Holbein, was removed by his father from Oxford because he was too taken with the study of Greek. Then an elective, Greek studies were thought by many to promote "dangerous modes of thinking." His father placed him in the Inns of Court to study law, and he ultimately rose to Lord Chancellor under Henry VIII. More was at ease with both the medieval thought-mode resting on church authority and with the new learning which sprang from the revival of classicism. While he supported many reforming practices, he could not forswear the pope. For his refusal, he was executed by Henry VIII and his head was "fixed upon London bridge." Legend holds it was recovered by his daughter and buried with her at St. Dunstan.

Henry VIII's tastes ran to letters and arts. He brought foreign scholars to his court, was a patron of the just-invented printing press, and was careful that his children had every advantage the new learning could offer.

But it was in legislation for the policing of the realm where Henry VIII's real legacy lies. Murderers had to be tried within a year and a day; access to the courts was given to the poor through writs at no cost; sheriffs were no longer allowed to issue fines unless in court; and juries were made available for trials. He organized the star chamber. Though later much-hated, in his day it was the only instrument to bring to justice barons, sheriffs, and others of authority whom the local courts were afraid to try. Henry was also interested in commerce and, while his mark here may not be great, he did lend to merchants and tradesmen when they were unable to get credit elsewhere.

Henry strengthened and enforced the laws against retainers. A great lord would retain persons in his service to do his bidding in war, in riots, or as witnesses in trials. These retainers were the soldiers in the War of the Roses. At Henry's insistence, the keeping of retainers was made a crime. The War of the Roses was the catalyst which permitted such a radical change. The antagonists, the houses of York and Lancaster, had used mercenaries trained in the Hundred Years War. These soldiers-for-hire changed sides at whim and brutally ravaged the countryside just as they had learned to do in Europe, a practice unusual to England except during the reign of William I. From the excesses of these soldier-retainers, the English developed a deep-seated hatred of professional soldiers which lasted for nearly four hundred years. As a happy consequence of Henry's radical new law, an enormous pool of talent, one which had previously been kept in idleness and mischief, was freed for profit and enterprise. As another profitable reward, the landed gentry replaced warring among themselves with a growing interest in the arts.

When Henry VII assumed the throne, England verged on anarchy. He left England "tame and orderly." He chose his ministers well, but did not allow anyone to be a "court favorite." A hard worker, he kept himself abreast of every ministry. He was careful with the realm's finances and had little need to call Parliament into session.

Though not much liked and not much mourned, he made a firm standing place for his son, Henry VIII, England's first sovran to be trained in the light of the Renaissance, and for his granddaughter, Elizabeth I.

Henry VIII

Henry VIII was received almost by acclamation. All his short-comings were excused by his youth and his much-admired gaming and sportsmanship. He was taller than his companions, a wrestler, a hunter, an archer, a versatile thinker, a skilled lutanist, and a fine singer. At first he showed no great interest in politics. The Spanish sovran, Ferdinand, seemed to treat England almost as a vassal state. **Catherine of Aragon**, Ferdinand's daughter, had previously been married to Henry's older brother Arthur. Upon Arthur's death, Ferdinand insisted she and Henry marry. They were married despite Henry's objection that Catherine had been married to his brother. At least in part, Henry's objection rested on canon law which prohibited such a union.

Ferdinand took Henry into a war with France, and Henry showed himself to be a worthy general. Ferdinand soon deserted him, so when Henry could work out a favorable treaty with France, he took England out of that war. Henry was an intelligent man possessed of great curiosity, and the escapade in France was just the trigger he needed to become an active sovran.

During his interlude away from Ferdinand, rumblings of divorce from Catherine were allowed to circulate throughout the realm, for she had not given him a live heir. These rumors did not abate until she bore him Mary and until his conflicts with Ferdinand were solved. Contemporaneously with these rumblings, **Cardinal Wolsey**, Henry's chief minister, fought mightily for papal consent of a divorce of Henry from Catherine. It would have been granted by Rome immediately, without years of back-and-forth bartering and ultimate rejection, had Ferdinand not been so influential in Rome.

Upon Ferdinand's death, Europe became a contested field between Charles V and Francis I, easily the two most powerful monarchs in Europe. England under Henry, with the conniving Wolsey, was for a time arbiter between the two. England had come that far.

Wolsey, however, was a problem. He had the tastes and desires of a prince, if not a king. He enjoyed palaces and every pleasure of the body while clothed in the red of a cardinal. Wolsey was an intemperate spendthrift whose profligacy was blamed for the difficulties Henry was to have with his Parliament. His loose fingers and his lusty appetite for carnal romping brought about his own downfall. But Wolsey held on long enough to solidify opposition to both himself and to the Roman church.

The Downfall of the Roman Church

Before we pass from Cardinal Wolsey, we must recognize his leniency towards, and perhaps his support for, church reforms. **Hugh Latimer**, at first a staunch papist, suddenly made an abrupt change to discard scholasticism and become a champion of the new learning. Rumors spread of the contents of his sermons. His bishop came unannounced to hear one, and when it was known he was in the congregation, Latimer sharpened the sermon especially for his bishop. Latimer was immediately forbidden to preach within the diocese. Wolsey, however, was sensitive to the new learning and authorized him to preach throughout England.

Prior to Latimer, ideas of church reform circulated secretly, principally through the works of Wycliffe. Through Latimer, those ideas had a full voice armed with the tongue of a skilled and nimble debater. After Henry VIII broke with the pope, Latimer, along with **Thomas Cranmer**, and Thomas Cromwell, was a chief advisor on religious matters to his court. For his work, Queen Mary had Latimer burned at the stake in 1555. It was said he "received the flame as it were embracing him. After he had stroked his face with his hands, and (as it were) bathed them a little in the fire, he soon died (as it were) with little pain or none."

While Henry was no Protestant, and his opposition to Martin Luther had earned him the title "defender of the faith" from Pope Leo X, it is doubtful that he was governed by any strong religious convictions. With the exodus of Wolsey and no binding ties to a church, the way was opened for laymen to move into positions of power unlike anything which had existed before in England. In time, Henry, with Parliament as his legislative partner, stripped the church of its enormous holdings and privileges. This action was not taken without real hardship and anxiety, especially in the north. The pomp and showmanship of religious services were the only diversions many people had from an otherwise dull life. Also some of these church-owned estates were in the hands of the friars, who had taken the vow of poverty. They were universally recognized as very tolerant and considerate landlords and were little more than the collectors of rents, at rates considered to be reasonable. Yet the people were aware that parish clerics were poorly trained and many kept mistresses, a practice so widespread that in 1518 Cardinal Wolsey had to publish an ordinance against "housekeepers." It was these conditions which made the populace sympathetic to Henry's break with the pope.

Over time, Henry stripped the ecclesiastic courts of their former authority. Almost of equal importance for the relief of his subjects, he stamped out the remaining claims of feudalism in the north and the west of England and Wales, parts of his realm where the royal writ had not previously run. With all his changes to English life, he possessed that marvelous sense to know when to stop and when to divert attention by rejoining European conflicts.

Opening the way for laymen to move into positions of power, as Henry had done, was an idea lost to the West since the rise of the Afro-Roman church. For this long span, few outside the church could read or write, and clerics were the cadre used to staff governments. The Renaissance, of course, had opened education to almost anyone, but outside of England the clerics continued as government operatives.

Following Wolsey's ouster, the church's hold on the offices of government was broken. **Thomas Cromwell** (1485?-1540) was a remarkable exemplar of the layman as civil servant. The son of a brewer, he could not get along with his ungovernable father, so he fled to Italy and became a soldier in the French Army. He was befriended by a Florentine banker, and, in turn, became an Antwerp merchant, and a London solicitor. He met Wolsey and was his advisor until Wolsey's fall. Through the Duke of Norfolk, he went into Henry's service. He rose to become secretary of state, was in charge of Henry's dismantling of the church properties, and finally was made Earl of Essex shortly before he was beheaded. He was a man of prudence, industry, and ability, and one who deserved a better fate. He never abused those under him and was driven by no force except to serve his master, He set the standard for civil service.

Cromwell is listed in Foxe's *Book of Martyrs* as a Protestant. He was certainly a diligent proponent of such Protestantism in the first test as adhering to the principle of sovran over church in matters of government. But he has been regarded as sacrilegious on the other test of scripture over church in matters of faith. In actuality, there is little to suggest he was of any religious temperament.

Given the church's diminished strength and increased opprobrium, lay people moved into government in numbers larger than those since the fall of the Roman empire. Henry's reign was the time for lay persons to learn the art of civil administration, to prepare for the reign of Elizabeth.

England Turns to the New World

Anyone who takes up a world globe, puts a finger on England, and measures out from that point to the different land masses scattered over the globe can see that England lies at the center. As the English have said, London's Picadilly Circus is the "center of the world." When Henry divorced Catherine, the resulting hostility put England in a different posture to the European continent. It slowly but surely made England turn her eyes away from the continent and to the New World. And England's gaze was never that of a looter as was Spain's, or as a keeper of a private game preserve as was Belgium's; its gaze was that of an investor. These were people accustomed to a good reward from crops or wool after a fair day's labor, and a people growing accustomed to investing that gain in enterprises not necessarily under their own management. This is a land becoming accustomed to its citizens making investments in all sorts of enterprises.

But England's location was simply a fact Henry was able to exploit in a new world climate by changing the attitude of the English for westward growth. Henry was an incarnation of Machiavelli's Prince. He saw himself and England as identical, and by a grand stroke of coincidence, they were. He was called "a despot under the forms of law." But a despot he was not: he did not break the law, but he had the skill to use the law to its fullest to exploit for his own greed for power. He strengthened and used Parliament to curb both the church and the remaining feudal barons. Parliament gave Henry largely what he wanted, yet Parliament owed its strength to him. Henry VIII was a remarkable combination of practicality and political perception, with an uncanny sense of self-restraint that made his hunger for power bearable. He became the focus of his people, and he made England a centralized state, the sort of state required for the coming age. A grand example of his strength was his ability to curb the Roman church, yet he did so in a way that avoided the religious civil wars like those which made deep scars across the face of Europe.

We noted earlier that Henry VII was the first to launch a vessel for the state. But it was his son, Henry VIII, to whom we must give credit for the birth of English naval power, so indispensable to England's future and to her place in the sun. According to Drake Corbett, "[T]he year 1545 best marks the birth of the English naval power." English sea power would ripen into the tools for Elizabeth's defeat of the Spanish Armada, for freeing the Netherlands, and for securing colonies in the western hemisphere and beyond.

Compulsory Public Education

Henry VIII created Trinity College at Cambridge in 1546, just as Wolsey had established Christ College at Oxford. Both were well endowed by their benefactors. None of the great English writers lived during Henry's reign, though **Sir Thomas More** acquired a reputation for his scholarship. Since Henry and his court were undeniably interested in letters and education, his reign made learning fashionable. Henry encouraged the translation of European writings into the vernacular, and these works became widely available.

John Colet organized a grammar school at his own expense next to St. Paul's Church, the first school not administered by a church. His teachings were based on a rational religious influence untainted by scholasticism. By his example, more schools were organized in the last years of Henry VIII's reign than in the preceding three centuries. Upon this foundation, the great middle class schools which would change the entire future of England were established.

No other people had such a wide chance of open opportunity so free of despotic oppression or governmental interference. Erasmus was quite impressed with the interest shown in education by persons so diverse in backgrounds. A great example of the width of this opportunity is **Ben Jonson**, the son of a bricklayer. As we shall see, the love of learning was the seed bed of a grand garden about to blossom in the reign of Elizabeth I.

Despite Henry's greed, his people thought well of him throughout his reign. His principle fault may well lie in this affection of his people which gave full rein to his extremely dominating personality. He was always true to a friend, such as Thomas Cranmer, but unforgiving and unrelenting to anyone who crossed or questioned him.

In the short reign of Henry's successor, Edward VI, Protestantism got a strong foothold in England. Edward was succeeded by Jane, queen for only ten days; she deserves mention because at age sixteen, she was a proficient reader of ancient Greek writings. During Mary's reign, the Roman church made an effort to return. According to Giovanni Micheli in *Relazione*, some have asserted that the reception given to the return of Romanism was proof of its popular support, but the Venetian Ambassador Micheli may have been closer to the mark when he said the English,

> would be full as zealous followers of the Mohammedan or Jewish religion did the king profess either of them, or command his subjects to do so; that, in short, they will accommodate themselves to any religious persuasion, but most readily to one that promises to minister to licentiousness and profit.

Henry VIII married six times to get a male heir, but his prize was the great Elizabeth I. Though the royal line had passed through females, no queen had ever ruled, and there was a real concern whether a queen would be accepted as sovran. The first, Mary, ruled by act of Parliament.

Elizabeth I

Elizabeth I boasted of being "mere English," and clearly she was the most English sovran since Harold. Elizabeth may be the most successful of English monarchs. Certainly she had the most difficult of tasks in a turbulent and changing time. With Edward, and more so during the reign of Mary, she learned to walk the finest of lines with her very life at stake for a misstep. Elizabeth resisted giving up the Protestant faith until required, and she bided her time as Mary, through Popish fanaticism, turned the realm against the Roman church, so much so that upon Mary's death, the Spanish king described the rejoicing for Elizabeth as "indecent." The people had reason to rejoice: during Mary's reign nearly 300 persons were burned at the stake on religious grounds, one of whom was Thomas Cranmer. In his *History of England*, Hume states that Erasmus wrote about the poverty and slovenly habits of her reign: "The floors are commonly of clay, strewn with rushes, under which lies unmolested an ancient collection of beer, grease, fragments, bones, spittle, excrements of dogs and cats, and every thing that is nasty."

Elizabeth, as no other, was able to control the wildly antagonistic factions and hostile people. She did not like the Roman church, which had declared her to be a bastard, nor did she like the unceremonious Protestants except the monarchical Lutherans, but they were not popular in England. She found comfort in Catholics who renounced Rome and she had to work with Protestants. Though not religious, she liked the forms and ceremonies of a religion as she felt they gave stability to the realm. Probably by Elizabeth's time, a foreign invasion on religious grounds was unlikely, but interference and intermeddling were rampant. With enormous skill, Elizabeth managed all these zealots and antagonists so that none of them got the upper hand and England was able to prosper. Under her care, religious toleration grew so that, ever after, a non-religious cause was assigned for all subsequent bloodlettings. This achievement was an accolade to her cunning.

As queen, Elizabeth had great prerogatives which she exercised freely, and on occasion, with real violence. Yet, she was careful not to intrude into the established liberties of her subjects and they, in turn, regarded her with affection. Truly she was able "to run with the hares and hunt with the hounds."

In the use of power, she was every bit as assertive as her father. She never shrank from using the star chamber. This court was composed of persons serving at her pleasure, but when the sovran was present, she had sole authority. Elizabeth had a court of high commission to judge heresies. Heresy has always been whatever the speaker made it out to be. She employed this power to suit her own ends.

In addition to these instruments of force, there was her right to declare martial law – a right which made the other powers seem pale by comparison. It was invoked at the sovran's pleasure for any civil disorder. Elizabeth used it against the importation of bulls and against unacceptable writings. No one had the right to question her imposition of martial law. Probably no sovran in Europe had such absolute power. Her possession of such an absolute power is a testimonial to the restraint of English sovrans.

Though she was to masculine of mind and temper to be as fetching to men as Mary, nevertheless, she was a master in handling suitors. This ability was as much a weapon in her arsenal as any other skill. She tempted them all and submitted to none. Elizabeth used her feminine wiles as a tool to conduct foreign affairs, with allusions of promises to first one, then another, as the political winds of Europe changed directions, yet she asserted all the while "England for the English."

Her first parliament repealed the prohibition against foreign ships bringing goods to English ports. The effect on trade was magnetic. By the ninth year of her reign, the Royal Exchange was established in London to handle the cloth and wool trade to Antwerp and to the Netherlands. In that same year efforts towards exploration and colonization began. These actions fixed England's right to participate in New World settlements despite the Roman pope's division of the world among his followers, Spain and France. These were the training years for the English seamen who, at every encounter with the Spaniards, acquitted themselves fittingly.

The success of Elizabeth's reign has to be credited with many accomplishments, many of which were made in the face of almost insurmountable odds. Her first years were consumed in nurturing her realm back to health after being laid waste by Mary. Yet from almost the beginning of her reign, her subjects, as privateers, brought home enormous loads of stolen treasure from foreign shipping and ports. These constant raids on foreign treasure required all the skill she could muster to assuage the princes of Europe, yet she kept Europe, and especially Spain, at bay until 1588 when she was ready. Only then did she let the Spaniards send their **Armada** to England's shores. Until that Armada arrived, Elizabeth was unable to afford the comforting diversion of foreign wars, which can be a welcomed release to homebound tensions.

An heir would have been a great asset to Elizabeth for the comfort of her subjects, but at least until the defeat of the Armada, her wiles as temptress may have been more valuable to her people. Her talent to balance competing forces, her ability (like her grandfather and father before her) to select able ministers, and her wisdom to keep those ministers at arm's length prompted Henry III of France to say that Elizabeth was "la plus fine femme du monde."

Throughout these Tudor reigns, two qualities of government distinguished it from those on the continent. There was very little interference in the day-to-day lives of ordinary persons. Being left alone was almost unheard across the channel. And, equally as important and unlike other western nations, this new-found and enormous wealth wrested from the Spaniards and the Dutch by privateers was not concentrated in the hands of a few. The persons who brought this wealth to England included any citizen who had, or could commander, his own vessel, and that vessel was often crewed by seamen working for a share of the prize. All this money was reverberating through a nation which had already shown a fascination with learning and had an aptitude for joint enterprise among the different classes of peoples.

It was during these years that England took her first laborious steps in the enterprise of trade as we know it today. While not nearly as rewarding as it was to become, its prize was enough to make persons of all ranks become passionately joined for a share of the profits. These profits served as another forceful mechanism to wear away class barriers.

In an earlier day the aristocrat would never have been in "mere trade." But the profits of this new trade forged a link between the aristocrat and the merchant. This linkage civilized the first and elevated the second. As a signal of the melding of the population, England developed an architectural style all its own. Descendants of feudal barons no longer constructed their manor houses as fortresses; should those manors have turrets and fortifications, they were merely adornments.

The Elizabethan style was said to be modeled from her initial, with turrets at each end and a large porch in the center. Changes also reached the individual farm, which became smaller. They required more intensive work, but their output per acre almost doubled. Farm cottages were made more secure and more comfortable.

Elizabethan Literature

The Elizabethan period is synonymous with great literature. The period of Elizabeth literature extends from More's Neo-Platonistic *Utopia* through the Calvinistic writings of Milton. This is the Renaissance come late from the continent but richer because of the delay. This immense flowering of literature was due to a political settlement reached over the great houses of England: religious peace with its mental release through the Anglican church, the widespread interest in education, and the diffusion of wealth among so many.

The English, ever a practical people, were never widely taken by their deeper, more philosophical, and religious writers. But when an English person did turn to the written word, there were plenty of an earth, homespun sort to please any appetite. The most noble writings of any time, in any culture, include those of **William Shakespeare,**

Edmund Spenser, and the **King James Bible**. These, as well as the works of many other contemporary writers, have been translated to other tongues and have never lost their popularity.

To this day the King James version of the bible is especially celebrated. While James encouraged this work, it was not, as the dedication asserts, one of which he was "the mover and author," nor was he resolute in faith or in its propagation. Mostly, he supported the Church of England because its stalwarts supported him. He would persecute persons of any faith should it serve his purpose or answer an indignity. Of authorship, that Bible was founded upon the Bishops' Bible of 1568, and from Cranmer's Bible, reaching back to Tyndale and to Wycliffe. The hallmark of all English translations since Wycliffe's, including the King James Bible, was to deviate as little as possible from what the people had become accustomed.

The lack of a true, rigid class and the intimacy of sovran and subject, which we have so often seen, affects these English writings. They have a natural, intimate style formed with virtually no governmental interference in literary efforts. They just seemed to bubble up out of the people. This natural flow contrasts starkly to both France and Germany. In France, what was good writing, just as what was acceptable art, style, and manners, was set by the ruling classes. The people followed the direction given by their leaders. (In our own time President Mitterand has stated that if the people had had the authority to accept or reject I. M. Pei's crystal addition to the Louvre, it would not have been accepted. This was, he said, an occasion when the people needed guidance.) In Germany, the educated, the writers and scientists, formed their own exclusive "clubs" into which the ordinary German was not welcome. When German science and writing were at their zenith, and equal to any, the German folk had no part in, or awareness of, this advancement.

With the defeat of the Armada, foreign threats against England were stilled, and the nation was bathed in a prosperity from which no one was excluded by any force outside himself. This prosperity nurtured the broadening of a base of people so that the English, though so few, could furnish the men and women who would be the bearers of English life to the entire globe. Before Elizabeth relinquished the throne, she was talking of "Britain for the British." In *Rise and Growth of the English Nation*, W.H.S. Aubrey has affectionately summed up her reign:

> Never was English monarch surrounded by such an illustrious band of statesmen and administrators. Never was a reign more renowned for its galaxy of literary splendor, for its merchant princes, and for its bold navigators, who by their enterprise and courage made the name of England famous across unknown seas and in distant lands. It was called, with pardonable exaggeration, the Golden Age and the Augustan Age of the country's history, filling "the spacious times of great Elizabeth with sounds that echo still." It formed the theme of Kenilworth, one of the greatest of Scott's romances. Men flourished of whom any nation and any period might well be proud.

In a real way these romantic words do sum up the Tudor's time of transition. A transition, with a momentary interruption by the Stuarts and the Cromwells, which brought the end to any vestiges of feudalism with only the word "county" left as its souvenir. It brought an end to any claims of temporal authority that may have once belonged to the church. These reigns trained laymen in the art of statecraft and invested them with the capacity to learn that rulers act only with the consent of the governed.

15 A CONSTITUTIONAL MONARCHY

The establishment of a constitutional government
of ministers appointed by the sovran upon the
approval of a popularly elected legislature.

It is as true about historical footsteps as it is of any we take: there are times we walk backwards. Perhaps, as Samuel Rogers suggested, "The good are better made by ill, As odors crushed are sweeter still," and so, these backward movements may be necessary. After the reign of Elizabeth, who died without heir, the Stuarts became the sovrans.

The reigns of the two James and two Charles, interrupted by Cromwell's interregnum, were not the best of times for England, but along the path some gems are to be found. Indeed, the Stuarts may have been indispensable to the more rapid confirmation of a constitutional monarchy.

James I, also James VI of Scotland, was not cut from English cloth. Resting on Old Testament mythology that God appointed kings, he brought to England a notion that he had some sort of the "divine right" to govern. As Green wrote in *A Short History of the English People,* James "destroyed that enthusiasm of loyalty which had been the main strength of the Tudor line." England may have appeared despotic at the death of Elizabeth, but England had no standing army, an indispensable tool of a despot. This lack of a means for coercion defeated James I before he could become a despot. And we should recall, Parliament's experiences had already included the overthrow of a church, establishing another, executing one ruler, declaring another illegitimate, and twice deposing of a monarch. Taken together, this history gave Parliament a great sense of authority, should it decide to act.

James' rule was marked both by religious persecutions and by an effort to suppress Parliament. Early in his reign he issued instructions describing the sort of person to be sent to Commons. He imposed a tax upon imports, claiming foreign trade to be outside the reach of Parliament. He ignored an unbroken rule since Edward I that taxes were imposed only by the House of Commons. Any idea of taxing trade was of enormous concern as commerce was beginning to grow by leaps. Trade was a growing source of income for an increasing number of persons. During this reign, the first American settlement was established in Virginia, and the East India Company was chartered. Had these ventures been bled by a rapacious monarch, they could have been destroyed. The king's only response was that his authority was absolute. Sovrans before the Stuarts had claimed their authority to be absolute, but, by this, earlier kings meant only their authority was beyond the influence of a foreign prince or a pope. No earlier ruler had ever regarded himself as beyond the reach of his ministers or Parliament.

Commons, in session after session, rebuked James. Commons declared it was "the indubitable right of the people of this kingdom not to be made subject to any punishment that shall extend to their lives, lands, bodies, or goods, other than such as are ordained by the common laws of this land, or the statutes made by their common consent in Parliament." The issue was joined but not resolved.

In his *History of the Reformation*, Burnett says of this James,

No king could be less respected, and less lamented at his death. England, which acted so great a part, and whose queen, Elizabeth, was the arbiter of Christendom and the wonder of her age, sank under his government into utter insignificance, and King James was the laughing-stock of his age. While hungry writers at home bestowed on him the most extravagant praises, all foreign countries looked upon him as a pedant without judgment, courage, and firmness, and as a slave of his favorites.

Charles I, his son, followed him to the throne. He was not content to merely succeed to all his father's ill will – he added to it. Charles was an egoist. As the Venetian Ambassador reported, "he was so constituted by nature that he never obliges anyone by word or act." When Parliament refused to appropriate money for him, he imposed his own taxes, his edict enforced by illegal arrests or by the quartering of troops in private houses until the tax was paid. Charles ultimately had to call Parliament into session and was forced to sign a "Petition of Right," in 1629, before he got his money. He immediately returned to autocratic rule. He twice more called Parliament into session. The first lasted twenty-three days and the second was in session for thirteen years, the **"Long Parliament."** At the last one, he crossed his Rubicon by going into forbidden territory, the House of Commons, looking for his enemies, and presuming to make demands. After a civil war, he surrendered in 1647, and in 1649 he was beheaded.

Oliver Cromwell, the idol of the army which had defeated Charles, became the leading voice of the parliamentary government which followed. He was a Puritan. Cromwell dissolved Parliament and became an autocrat himself, a king without the title. While Cromwell was honest and unselfish, he was repressive and intolerant.

Cromwell's success was in foreign affairs. He chose France's side against the Spaniards, who were the models of the sort of religious repression and intolerance imposed by the Roman church, just as Cromwell was the exemplar of the puritanical kind. He led England to victory in the commercial wars with Holland, and, for the first time since the Plantaganets, England was a European power of the first rank.

On his death, Cromwell's son, Richard, succeeded him. However, Richard failed. Parliament restored the monarchy with **Charles II**, another Stuart, on the throne.

As Napoleon had said of the Bourbons, the Stuarts "learned nothing and forgot nothing." Judged by his character and by his foreign policy, Charles II's reign might be the worst of all England sovrans. Wrong-doing, weakness, and confusion were its hallmarks. His treatment of others could be contemptible. Taxation for defense was increased, but security was reduced. Not only could Holland's ships circle the island at will but they could sail up the Thames and fire on the nation's arsenals. England could not have been held in less esteem. It was beset by unprincipled ministers, a wasteful court, and an incompetent king, a situation exacerbated by a plague and the great fire of London which destroyed the nation's monuments.

Reforms in Government

But all the forces of the English were at work as part of an irrepressible intellectual growth. Such growth occurred despite the heavy hand of government, a hand more likely to retard then aid such growth. During Charles' reign the accomplishments by Parliament are as great as in any similar period in the history of England. An enforceable Habeas Corpus Act was passed so that, should anyone be arrested, there was a real means for immediate inquiry of its correctness. The writ allowing the church to tax itself was abolished so that thereafter it was required to submit to legislative assessments of its properties. A writ allowing church officials to force a person to incriminate himself was abolished. The House of Lords lost original jurisdiction in civil cases. Taxation was placed exclusively in the hands of elected officials with only Commons having the authority to originate a money bill. A statute of frauds and perjuries gave real security to private property.

And a law restricting unlicensed printing was allowed to lapse, ushering in freedom of the press, a notion abhorred by both king and church.

Charles II's proclivity towards unrestrained debauchery made him resist any sort of control. He expressed open contempt of clergy because they opposed his insatiable indulgences. His ecclesiastic appointments were given to those least gifted in intellect or ability. But his opposition to the clergy did, fortunately, require that he support **Thomas Hobbes**, an active opponent to the church. Hobbes had one of the ablest minds of his day. Together by chance, if not design, these two acted in concert to further weaken the grip of the church, that medieval foe to intellectual growth.

Though Charles II's reign saw little literary accomplishment, **Francis Bacon's** seeds of intellectual freedom began to grow just as soon as society could recover from the civil war and Cromwell's governance. Two giants of this time, casting shadows well beyond their own days, were **Issac Newton** and **Christopher Wren**. Newton led the vanguard of the world's scientific knowledge. In all the annuals of human existence, it is doubtful anyone will match Wren's opportunity, coupled with his ability, to create so many monuments. And in the last year of Charles' reign, **Edward Heming** began lighting the streets of London.

In *The History of England*, Hume, remarking on another's comparing Charles to Rome's ancient and tyrannical Tiberius, said,

> The emperor seems as much to have surpassed the king in abilities, as he falls short of him in virtue. Provident, wise, active, jealous, malignant, dark, sullen, unsociable, reserved, cruel, unrelenting, unforgiving; these are the lights under which the Roman tyrant has been transmitted to us; and the only circumstance in which it can justly be pretended he was similar to

Charles is his love of women, a passion which is too general to form any striking resemblance, and which that detestable and detested monster shared also with unnatural appetites.

James II followed his brother Charles II to the throne. Of James and his father, Charles I, Hallam wrote in his *Constitutional History of England*, "They were both equally unfitted for the condition in which they were meant to stand – the limited kings of a wise and free people, the chiefs of the English commonwealth." Three days after his ascension to the throne, James ordered the collection of illegal levies. Then James, with all his badges of kingship, went to mass in a Roman church, an illegal act, to flaunt his arbitrariness and his bigotry. Without pause, he sent an emissary to Rome to pursue England's return to the church of Rome. The pope was more prudent and counselled James to act with caution. He would not be dissuaded. His consuming passion was to reestablish the Roman church in England. He asked the Spanish ambassador, "Is it not the custom in Spain for the king to consult with his confessor?" The ambassador replied, "yes, and it is for this very reason our affairs succeed so ill." Later, because he had allied himself with the king of France, an enemy of the pope, the Roman bishop would not help him. Towards the end of his short reign, James attempted to affect some degree of religious toleration. For this act, he was deserted by the English clergy. After a tumultuous three years scarred by religious conflicts, **William of Orange** was invited to England. When William landed with his army, James fled to France, and Parliament declared the throne vacant. Parliament ruled for a short while and then, by contract, established William of Orange and his wife, Mary, of the house of Stuart, as joint monarchs. This was a **"Glorious Revolution."**

A Return to Constitutionalism

Eighty-six years from Elizabeth to William and Mary, eighty-six years to remind the English only they could preserve their individuality. The events of these years confirmed that the sovran sat on the throne at the pleasure of the parliament, that the king was subject to, not independent of, the law. During these years there had been continual efforts by these Stuart kings to levy taxes, to maintain a standing army, and to deny free right of debate in parliament, each decree enacted without the consent of Parliament. But the laws holding each to be illegal, despite violations, remained intact.

During those eighty-six years, many who were likely to complain either went to, or were sent to, the New World. Several attempts to colonize North America had failed because the wrong people were sent. What was needed were workers, but dandies and gentlemen were the settlers. **John Smith** alone saved Virginia as he struggled to make the colonists work, soothed their quarrels, and gave them heart. With each returning vessel, which he was ordered to fill with gold or goods, he pleaded for workers. He got more dandies, but he struggled and he saved Virginia.

The historian Buckle wrote in his *History of Civilization in England,*

> It is, indeed, difficult to conceive the full amount of the impetus given to English civilization by the expulsion of the House of Stuart. Among the most immediate results, may be mentioned the limits that were set to the royal prerogative; the important steps that were taken towards religious toleration; the remarkable and permanent improvement in the administration of justice; the final abolition of a censorship over the

press; and, what has not excited sufficient attention, the rapid growth of the great monetary interests by which…the prejudices of the superstitious classes have in no small degree been counter-balanced. These are in the main characteristics of the reign of William III as a reign often aspersed, and little understood, but of which it may be truly said, that, taking its difficulties into due consideration, it is the most successful and the most splendid recorded in the history of any country.

Upon the accession of William III and Mary, Parliament granted funds for only one year, but refused to make a grant to the crown for their entire reign, though this had been the custom. The sovran no longer had the luxury of calling Parliament, getting a lifetime authority for revenues, then never calling Parliament again short of a calamity. From the rule of only annual revenues, the king must call Parliament into session every year. Parliament also insisted that each of the grants made had to be for particular services. These may not have been new ideas, but until that time they had not been enforced. They were never abandoned. These rules about the revenue were a great shield against corrupt or errant expenditures by a sovran.

When William began his reign, he, like his predecessors, called persons for posts on his privy counsel. But, William, unlike the others, sought a representative group of both Whigs and Tories, though weighted towards the Whigs as they had supported him. It did not work. There were squabbles and jealousies among the members. William wanted his ministers to "act in party," and to submit their wills to a general agreement. He conceived he could best carry out his concepts with the party that had supported him from the first. From his privy council, there was established, according to Waller's *Parliamentary History*, a cabinet, "a ministry, whose possession of power under the authority of the sovran, and with the command of a parliamentary majority."

The administration of justice was made more secure by making judges' tenure *quamdiu bene se gesserint*, for "as long as he shall behave himself." In 1694 the **Bank of England** was chartered to answer a need for money for the military. Its organization and ability to function were a testament that commerce had become quite lucrative, and perhaps more significant, the holders of this wealth were willing to invest it beyond their own sight. It opened an entirely new landscape for business opportunity and the general diffusion of wealth and knowledge. It was part of the realization of Adam Smith's teaching that there need not be a perpetual group of poor persons.

Efforts were made for religious toleration. May's *Constitutional History of England* reports that with the passage of the Toleration Act, though it "repealed none of the statues requiring conformity with the church of England [it] exempted all persons from penalties, on taking an oath of allegiance and supremacy, and subscribing to an oath against transubstantiation." Toleration was still withheld from Roman Catholics and Unitarians. A contemporary writer expressed it as an effort to safely navigate "between the meretricious gaudiness of the church of Rome and the squalid sluttery of fanatical conventicles." In reality, the ideas of toleration, in William's more conciliatory view, were premature. Despite these sluggish steps, society was moving in the direction of toleration, and there could be little doubt that full toleration of religious thought would follow.

History itself was a travelling companion of religious freedom. The existence of varied beliefs, with a right to question, are indispensable to any sense of historical perspective. As recently as the seventeenth century, the recordings of historical facts are often like childish accounts of a writer's narrow view. Divine direction or intervention was ascribed as the cause of every event. Wars were not lost because of lack of supply or training, but because it was a deity's will. Medieval writings were usually in a "chronicle" form, but the writer had no appreciation of what information to retain or reject. As one reads them, the repeating refrain is "credulity." Writers accepted the most preposterous explanations and causes as fact. History can have no form, no selection, and no artistic beauty of what has gone before until there is doubt. Doubt has to be accepted, and even encouraged, to have any fair gaze at what has gone before. Doubt requires toleration, and toleration requires religious choice. In *Somer's Tracts*, Scott speaks of the persecutions by the Church of England against its opponents:

> This is the stale pretense of the clergy of all countries, after they have solicited the government to make penal laws against those they call heretics or schismatics, and prompted the magistrates to a vigorous execution, then they lay all the odium on the civil power, for whom they have no excuse to allege, but that such men suffered, not for religion, but for disobedience of the laws.

A masterpiece of William's reign was **The Settlement Act** of 1701, which fixed succession to the throne to a Protestant. More significant by far, however, was that the Act fixed the power of the Parliament as the guardian of its own, and the people's rights and privileges. This statute marks the firm mooring of constitutional monarchy. Hereafter, only George III will intemperately challenge Parliament with his notion that Royal Prerogative extended uninterruptedly to foreign domains, but when George lost the American colonies, this last pretense of sovran supremacy was annihilated. What was constructed in William's reign has served as a model for national legislatures around the world.

To appreciate these accomplishments, we can look at England's chief rival, France. The pernicious weed of absolutism found fertile soil in the Bourbons just as it did on the Stuarts. The English pulled it out by its roots. In contrast, absolutism grew unabated in France, with a three-house legislature an ineffective weapon against it. Three houses of a legislature cannot agree on anything. Only the fiery holocaust of the French Revolution and its aftermath stemmed the growth of absolutism.

Sometimes to understand an act we should know the actor: Mary died in 1694 and William lived until 1702. On his last morning he called for his great friend and supporter, Bentinck, with whom he had shared every mortal grief and joy. Bentinck leaned close to his king, but William could speak no more. The king took Bentinck's hand, drew it to his heart, and died. When he was laid out, a small black ribbon was found next to his body. In it was a gold ring with a lock of Mary's hair.

Establishing a Ministerial Government

Parliamentary government reached maturity under George I. One of his first acts was to dismiss the Tory ministers because they had supported the Stuarts. While his ministers were Whigs, the Commons was composed of a Tory majority. In time it was realized that union between the Commons and the ministers was essential if the government were to function. An accord called for the sovran to appoint the ministers, but in order to serve, the ministers had to be approved by a majority of Commons.

With annual revenues and annual sessions of Parliament, and ministers approved by Commons, constitutional government was formed. It needed only time to set. George I's reign was a time of peace and prosperity. It was the time when a great and prosperous middle class grew firm roots. It was a time for this new constitutional government to become at home with itself. Both George I and George II were ideal for those years. They were not English. They cared little for England, as their hearts were in their German provinces. As has been correctly said, "the King reigns but does not govern." The parliament was allowed to ripen so as to be able to withstand the last assault.

16 EXPANSION

The formation and loss of an empire, and the assembly of another.

In the last years of Elizabeth, England had no possessions outside Europe. Despite all the efforts of Drake, Gilbert, and Raleigh, no colony existed anywhere under the English flag. There was no Calais. There was no Great Britain. Scotland was a separate kingdom. The English ruled in Ireland, but they were aliens in a land of people who had reverted almost to being wild tribesmen.

The internal unification of England after the Stuarts came in the reign of William III. James II, with the aid of the Bourbons, invaded Ireland to rid England of the "Usurper" William. He lost, of course, but he left William with the task of breaking the will of the Irish resistance which James had provoked. But this was only one of many dissenting groups spawned by the Stuarts. The Stuarts had separated the people within the English boundaries into factions along every possible seam: religionists, absolutists, parliamentarians, and social classes. When William took the throne, he watched them all squabble and feud among themselves, but sagely, he never took sides. Always an outsider, and never really at home, but by his judicious behavior he did quell the feuds and achieved what he wished: a debating parliament with the ability to compromise, and a nation not riven with ideologic cleavages.

Foundation of Great Britain

The internal union that became Great Britain was completed in **Anne's** reign. The two nations of England and Scotland had one sovran beginning with James I, but the Scots remained jealously independent. Not until 1707 were tempers cooled off enough to agree on a joint parliament. After years of conflict, then success over the Scots, an English supporter named a flower "Sweet William." A Scotsman replied by naming a weed "Stinking Willie." The traditions of the Highlanders were similar to those of the English. Browne's *History of the Highlands* relates that a highland chief had "no particular power and no limitations, but, if irregular, [was] easily restrained by the elders of the tribe. The chief had immediate need to gather as many followers as possible which raised the clansman in his own estimation." And, with the coming expansion, the Scots' intelligence, thrift, and stoic ways made them immensely valuable for colonial service.

The first expansion beyond the seas was with the charter to The Virginia Company in 1606. By 1900, her domains would extend around the globe. They included, disregarding military and naval stations, the Dominion of Canada, the West Indian Islands with settlements in Central and South America, South African possessions, the Australian group including New Zealand, and India. They were populated with over ten million people of European blood. And, in that span, England had lost one empire and gained another.

The eighteenth century was essentially one of unity within England itself. There was one long reign of **George III** with his feckless Lord North as chief minister, but there also a long ministry under the most able **William Pitt**, later Lord Chatham.

The great events of this time of expansion, actually from 1688 to 1815, were wars, a second Hundred Years War. Seven wars occurred, the first beginning in 1689, as a part of England's "Glorious" Revolution, and lasting until 1697. The second war is called the War of Spanish Succession, in which **Marlborough** achieved his remarkable victories. It was fought from 1702 to 1713 and spawned a longer peace resting solely on the exhaustion of the parties, not on resolution of any controversy.

In 1739, there was the War of Jenkins' Ear. Jenkins was the master of a trading vessel. His ship was boarded outside Jamaica. Though no smuggling was proven, a Spanish captain tore off his ear and told him to take it to his king with the warning that were the king there the same would happen to him. (Incidentally, Jenkins always carried his ear with him, wrapped in cotton. Everywhere he went he would show it to anyone who would look. In truth, there have been questions raised about the way in which he lost his ear.) This war mushroomed into the War of Austrian Succession and continued until 1749. Then came the Seven Year's War, a war promoted by the colonies and the only one into which they did not have to be dragged. This war is remembered for the Battle of Abraham's Height and the death of Wolfe. Next was the American War, truly a civil war in England, with persons sympathetic to each side on both sides of the Atlantic.

There followed another war with France from 1793 to 1803, then another in quick succession from 1803 until the Battle of Waterloo in 1815. Between the wars, **George Washington** had his battle at Fort Duquesne while fighting under the Union Jack. There was the battle causing the death of Braddock, and, half way around the world, Clive's battles in India. These last battles were fought in the absence of a declared war.

These wars and these battles had two common threads. Each of them, at least at the end, occurred between England and France. Each of them were fought over possession of the New World or India, and was concerned with trade and commerce.

In each step of England's expansion through America and India, France was there. When England settled Virginia and New England, France was settling Acadia and Canada. When William Penn was organizing Pennsylvania, La Salle was going on discovery and claim from the Great Lakes to the mouth of the Mississippi. France got Louisiana in 1683 and closed the back door to England.

The exploration and conquest of India was a French idea. The French got there first. The drive of Clive, Wellesley, Minto, and Hastings was more in answer to a fear of the French than any desire for trade. They were concerned with French intrigue and French gold.

The War of Spanish Succession was about trade. It was about blocking England from any trade in the New World. Napoleon took his war to Egypt, not because it was a prize, but to block the English and regain possession of India. Napoleon continued with his dream of India in his second war with England. The second time around he was not as bold; his first target was Malta. Had he won, he would have had a stepping stone to Egypt, and, then, on to India. His seizures of Spain and Portugal, each with New World possessions, confirm his interest in colonies and possessions. The war of 1793 was England's revenge for its lost of the American colonies in the American war, when, in the words of Cowper, France "picked the jewel out of England's crown."

The years between 1740 to 1783 were a time of change in relative strengths between these two European powers. The Seven Years War had started badly, but when the Whig William Pitt took over the war ministry, this incomparable leader infused England's forces with his own sense of patriotism and destiny. As prizes for victory over France, England received Nova Scotia, Canada, all the land between the Alleghenies and the Mississippi River, and India. From Spain came Florida.

England lost its war with France in 1783, ending with the Treaty of Paris. Though not then understood, the independence of the **United States** was not a victory for France or for any other colonial power. First, the former American colonials were English persons. English citizens continued to have investments in, and much goodwill towards, the people of the United States. Trade and emigration to America continued just as it had before. Second, the revolution provided a good example to other colonial powers that their colonists too could be free of their European overlords.

After the setback of the Treaty of Paris, England lost some of its enthusiasm. The English knew America was not plucked by the French, but it was thrown away by George III and his Lord North. Many English, especially those who supported the American colonies, referred to the American War as "the King's War." In this "king's war" Parliament knew it could also have been as much at peril as the American colonies if the king had won. This fear brought applause for each American victory from a fine array of Whig talent, including Pitt, Fox, and Burke. Incidentally, George III's intense hatred of Americans did not end with the war. In his *Works*, **John Adams** reports that in 1786, when he and **Thomas Jefferson** paid an official courtesy visit to King George in his palace, George acted with great incivility towards both of these gentlemen.

Edmund Burke, ever practical, softened the sting by suggesting expediency does not make correctness. Burke said if England had the authority to tax the colonists, as asserted by the king, such a tax was to bring only discord and rebellion. It was not proper to use the authority. Burke's literary skills relied not on the French jargon about "liberty and equality" as the Americans employed, but rested on reasonableness. His arguments found favor in England. Burke knew, as Turgot said, that "colonies are like fruits till they ripen."

Edmund Burke cannot be passed lightly. Robert Hall said of his mind: "The excursions of his genius are immense. His imperial fancy has laid all nature under tribute, and has collected riches from every scene of the creation, and every walk of art." He was at home with groups as diverse as artists and lawyers, a keen student of the derivation of languages before such study was thought of value, and he anticipated the thoughts of Adam Smith when Smith made his first trip down to London. Along with social philosophy, he appreciated the physical sciences. All these he could blend at will, with clear expression, to seek a practical solution, or, as Burke would say, a solution "adjusted by human nature." He was in the Commons for thirty years, but never held a ministry; yet, he was an effective counterweight to the delusions of George III. George needed a counterweight. The *Jefferson Cyclopedia* states that Jefferson wrote of the king, "Our friend George is rather remarkable for doing exactly what he ought not to do."

In advance of his contemporaries, Burke advocated freedom of trade, the right of worship for religious dissenters, reform of the laws respecting debtors, reform of the penal code, abolition of the slave trade, and correcting tenures of judges.

The American war did teach the English they could not have a mere mechanically forced union if England were to succeed with its empire. It would have to be a union of states. England received Canada from France in 1763, and in 1780 Cornwallis surrendered to the Americans. In 1791 Canada was given the right to reject any law passed in Parliament which affected Canada. Such a timely grant to the American colonies would have avoided America's quest for independence.

England's second empire was spread across North and South America, Africa, Asia, Australia with New Zealand, and little points of land like Gibraltar, Malta, the Caribbean Islands, Malaysia and literally every corner of the globe. England invested itself in each possession to make all of it a great trading area, bringing to mind the breadth of empire which had previously belonged only to Rome, but this one was of greater riches.

In that trading empire which was Rome, one could travel to its furthermost reaches and be understood by speaking Greek. In England's empire, the language was English.

17 EMANCIPATION

Freeing the mind to pursue thoughts
for the betterment of mankind and
to seek its own curiosities.

True freedom comes from within. Others, whether governments or individuals, can do little more than preclude, or remove, barriers from an individual's path. Ideally, all barriers, save only those necessary to grant each person equal access, should be shunned. We have seen some pass away. During the reigns of the Tudors, feudalism (both baronial and clerical) was put to rest, and the eyes of England were moved from Europe to gaze across the sea. Sea trade, in privately owned vessels, crewed by adventurers seeking a part of the spoils, brought riches to classes which had not before been touched by wealth. The reign of the Stuarts saw the beginnings of rewarding foreign settlements and the growth of commerce.

During the time of George III, **James Watt** perfected the steam engine. Before this engine, all power was supplied by animals, wind, or water. The making of goods was essentially the same as it had been for centuries. Cottage "factories" made goods for the local area only. If too much of a product was made, there was no way to get it to different markets. There was no transportation. There was no communication but that carried on the back of a horse or the leg of a pigeon. The steam engine was first used in mining; then it was employed in textile mills and used to power vessels and pull railroad trains. After that it reached factories and was employed in limitless ways. The changes wrought by the steam engine compare with any in the entire history of human enterprise.

In 1767, **James Hargreaves** invented a spinning jenny which would make ten threads at one time from either raw cotton or wool.

Two years later, **James Arkwright** made a spinning jenny which was driven by water power rather than by foot pedals. Later the capacity was increased to make two hundred threads at one time. This development meant a loom of greater capacity was needed. **Edmund Cartwright** invented that. These new machines went hand-in-glove with steam power. All this cotton, wool, thread, and cloth trade congested the canals of Britain. The answer came when the steam engine used in the textile industry was put into a vessel. In America, **Robert Fulton's** *Clermont* travelled the 150 miles from New York to Albany in thirty-two hours. It proved the practicality of this form of locomotion.

The mining industry had learned long before that laying tracks along the mine floor allowed draft animals to pull much larger loads through the mines by eliminating the resistance, or friction, of the ground. By 1813, a locomotive, **"Puffing Billy,"** was made. The next year saw a better one, pulling coal at three miles per hour. The **"Rocket"** was able to travel at thirty miles per hour by 1830.

A substantial reason for the defeat of the French at Waterloo was the strength of this industrial production. The Industrial Revolution in England was far advanced over that in France.

People left their farms; they acquired new ideas, and some wealth, or the knowledge of what wealth could bring to their lives. In 1776 **Adam Smith** published his *Inquiry into and the Nature and Causes of the Wealth of Nations*. His work is the foundation stone for a political economy, the sort of economy which includes the developed world as we know it today. Prior to this publication, it was a common belief, resting on church "truths," that there must be poor people in any society. It was expectable and correct, or unavoidable, that some persons would be destitute. Before Smith's work, there was a truism that a nation's wealth was measured by its treasury. This concept encouraged a state to be selfish, to look inward, as each nation's wealth was measured by the morning's counting of the coin in the realm.

Adam Smith held the factory workers and farm hands were also consumers. A factory could increase its output and its profits by selling its production to those who worked in factories. It was even desirable that those persons have wealth in order to purchase the factory's output to increase the wealth of the nation. This was a startlingly different notion. It was one which lifted enormous barriers from the backs of ordinary persons. Suddenly they could be counted as a source of wealth, as a valuable commodity. This was the siren-call for mass production and its catalyst, advertising.

Couple this notion of worker-consumer with Smith's other idea that the wealth of a nation is measured by its means of production, and the effect is synergistic. It means trade balances: if sales enjoy increasing levels, but are offset with loans (which are sales of a commodity too), a nation has a mechanism for prosperity. He also explained that activities such as travel by tourists add to a nation's wealth.

If any worker can be a customer of a factory, and, in addition, any worker anywhere in the world can be a customer of that same factory, the outcome is the **Industrial Revolution**.

Tie that to the lesson England learned from the loss of the American colonies: colonies, and an empire, are a collection of states. The Industrial Revolution transformed the British Empire into a collection of producers and consumers spread around the globe so there are English consumers always in the sun's full ray.

But factories make contradictions: a factory changes the work. In a cottage factory, a cobbler made a complete pair of shoes with satisfaction and pride. In the new mechanized factory, a worker might cut out tongues for shoes all day, every day. The worker got bored and wanted a shorter workday. But a longer day meant greater wages and more opportunities to buy the output of factories.

And factories were the pied piper to country folk. They came to the cities. They crowded into the cities. Factories spawned two groups: workers and capitalists. Each year saw the owner driven harder for profits, and the worker driven harder by need. Women and children were brought in by opportunity and forced to compete with one another through necessity.

Any reasonable chance for gradual reform had to wait for the horrid pictures painted by the French Revolution to fade. Those with any wealth were frightened by the wanton bloodshed and destruction of property which occurred in France. Conditions in the English factory got worse. This contradiction was kept in place by a parliament which could no longer pretend to be representative with the stunning migrations after the invention of the steam engine. The Parliament, then in the hands of the Tories, would not help.

Parliamentary Reform

Change was forced by the second French Revolution of 1830. The Bourbons were returned to the French throne after the Bonapartes. They tried to restore absolutism. Parisians took to the streets. The Bourbon government failed. Louis Phillipe was crowned after he swore to uphold the constitution. The clarion ring for freedom sounded by this uprising echoed across Europe. It was heard in England.

The most important reform was for Parliament to reform itself. Before the introduction of any bill to reform the Parliament, there were 489 members in the House of Commons from England. Each county had either one or two delegates. Boroughs may, or may not, have been given a burgess at time of creation, but only two had been given since 1625. Ten southern counties with one-quarter the population had almost half the votes. Some boroughs elected their members by vote of its mayor and alderman, while the ordinary citizen had no vote. Some large cities, such as Birmingham, had no member. The polls were open for fifteen days and bribery for votes was rampant. Anyone not a member of the Church of England could not vote or hold public office.

The poor and disheartened rose up under the prodding of **William Corbett** and his publication titled *The Weekly Political Register*. He cajoled and badgered, even reducing the cost of his paper to reach more people; he was unrelenting. The persons to whom he addressed his call had no vote. They could only take to the streets and petition. After George III died in 1820, there was some sense of reform developing, but the government was still in the hands of the Tories. Yet breaches were occurring. In 1828, the Test Act was repealed. Under this law, if one was unable to pass religious tests, to prove adherence to the Church of England, such person could not hold a public office of trust. The next year, the Catholic Relief Bill was passed, which permitted Roman Catholics to hold all but the very highest offices. Additional reforms occurred in areas of commerce, and the penal code. At the time, there were over one hundred offenses punishable by death, including picking another's pocket or defacing Westminster bridge.

George IV died in 1830, William IV was crowned, and the Whigs came to power in parliament. **Earl Grey**, a long-time advocate of reform, was elected prime minister.

The first reform bill was introduced in 1831. It was for the redistribution of seats in Commons. It was written to strip tiny towns, called "rotten boroughs," of their seats and make a fair re-allocation of them among the cities. Its reach amazed everyone.

Hansard's *Parliamentary Debates* reveal that the sponsor of the bill, **Lord Russell**, argued that an outsider, after hearing of England's unparalleled prosperity, its citizens' pride in their enlightenment and freedom, and its regular elections, would be astounded at the actual election process:

> What then would be his surprise, if he were taken by his guide, whom he asked to conduct him to one of the places of election, to a green mound and told, that this green mound sent two Members to Parliament – or, to be taken to a stone wall, with three niches in it, and told that these three niches sent two Members to Parliament – or, if he were shown a park, with many signs of flourishing vegetable life, but none of human habitation, and told that this green park sent two Members to Parliament? But his surprise would increase to astonishment if he were carried into the North of England, where he would see large flourishing towns, full of trade and activity, containing vast magazines of wealth and manufactures, and were then told that these places had no Representatives in the Assembly which was said to represent the people.

A bitter, acrimonious debate followed. According to Valentine's *Half Hours of English History*, The Duke of Buckingham wrote,

> The most exciting language was freely used, and a disposition shown to resort to violence. Indeed, the Marquis of Londonderry and other noblemen who had the manliness to express their opinions, as they had a constitutional right to do, in their place in parliament, were savagely assaulted by the mob. The example of London rioting and outrage spread to the provinces. in Derby, the town goal and the houses of

many respectable inhabitants were demolished. At Nottingham the ancient castle, the residence of the duke of Newcastle, was destroyed.

The bill was defeated. Parliament was dissolved. An election was held, and the Whigs came back stronger than before. A second reform bill, much like the first, was introduced. The Tories were dogged and persistent. They spoke to the issue an inordinate number of times. It passed Commons but was quickly defeated in the House of Lords.

Three months later, in December 1831, the bill was introduced in Commons for a third time. After these same Tory tactics, it was passed in March. The Lords were likely to kill it again. The only solution was to appoint enough new Lords to change the balance of power, but the king refused. When Grey resigned, the King asked Wellington, a Tory, to form a new government, but he could not do so. Grey was reappointed with a signed paper that said, "The King grants permission to Earl Grey and his Chancellor, Lord Brougham, to create such a number of peers as will be sufficient to insure the passing of the Reform Bill." The threat was enough, and the bill passed the House of Lords. In *Half Hours of English History*, Valentine reports that Robert Raikes, the founder of Sunday schools recorded, "December 3. – The king came up to town from Brighton, and signed the proclamation for dissolving the present parliament, and assembling the new on the 29th of January, 1833. From this day commences a new era for England."

In step with the Reform Act was the Municipal Corporations Act. As we have seen, in England since its earliest days, cities with separate charters have been undeniable foundation stones to the freedom of the English, who learned to administer and manage their own affairs in the local cities and parishes. Only the English have this centuries-old national tradition of local governments drawing their own rules, assessing and collecting their own taxes, and discussing their own business, not just in a few cities, but in hundreds of towns and parishes scattered across the width of England. With all these changes and a transient population seemingly awash across the entire state, local governments fell in corruption. Some became dispensers of patronage, whether clerical or lay, to their own pleasure. Neglect of proper functions of police and public administration was not uncommon. Funds were often wasted "in greasy feasts and revelry." Correction was granted in the Commons but slowed in the upper chamber. But it could not be denied for long.

Other reforms followed, and expectably so. In quick succession, the slave trade was abolished, child labor laws were enacted to prevent the employment of those under nine, and regulations were created for workers from nine to twelve: they could not be worked more than eight hours each day. It is one of the anachronisms of the machine age that simple, repetitive factory work can often be done by children just as readily as by adults, but they are paid much less than adults. Another reform involved the custody of children. Before the advent of child labor laws, custody was routinely given to the father in parental custody actions. After these laws were enacted, custody was increasingly awarded to the mother because children were no longer as great an economic asset.

In 1837, Victoria came to the throne. Though Carlyle called her "poor little queen," she reveled in her new position. She decided the question of her marriage by summoning her cousin Albert of Saxe-Coburg into her presence and offering him her hand. Afterward she said it was "a nervous thing to do." She added it was necessary as "he would never presume to take such a liberty." Sir Robert Peel said, "She is as full of love as Juliet." Their union was of pure affection and their views were in perfect harmony.

Electoral Reform

But perfect harmony did not yet include the workers as part of the electorate. Before reform, Cambridge, with 20,000 persons, had only 102 voters. In December, 1836, a pamphlet, *The Rotten House of Commons*, pointed out that of over six million adult males, only 839,519 were voters. In 1838 a petition demanded that every adult male be given the vote, that voting be secret, and that members of Commons be paid. The last was urged because otherwise only the wealthy could afford to sit. This petition was repeated in 1839, in 1842, and in 1848. Nothing came of these efforts.

Reform turned to removing trade barriers against the importations of foodstuffs and grain, the **"Corn Laws,"** and improving working condition in factories. The repeal of the Corn Laws was quite significant as it was these restrictions on importation of grains which had, for so long, protected the income of the landed gentry. With their repeal, the lot of the ordinary English person was improved, and England advanced further along the road to free trade.

By 1866 voter reform become an irresistible issue. The next year a reform bill was passed to extend the vote to every householder, and every tenant of one year's occupancy. It was then thought to be so broad that Lord Derby called it a "leap into the dark," and another member said it was like "shooing Niagara."

Parliamentary reform was substantially completed with the Reform Act of 1867 by making it apparent that Commons were dominant over the House of Lords. In *Parliamentary Reform*, Bagehot indicates that the Lords had to yield "whenever the opinion of the Commons is also the opinion of the nation."

While every adult male worker had the right to vote in 1867, that right, to be of value to the nation, required an educated electorate. England had a long-standing tradition that education was not a duty of the state. By tradition since the fall of the Roman empire, western states had left the matter of education to churches except at the college level.

The Growth of Public Education

In England, public education below the university level was deplorable when compared to that in some other European states. The one exception was boarding schools. The strength of these schools rested on the work of **Thomas Arnold**, 1795-1842, built on Colet's beginnings. but since Colet, schools had been neglected and had become distinguished more for flogging than teaching. A growing and prosperous middle class demanded better educational facilities. Because the railroad was sufficiently developed, it was acceptable these schools be "non-local." Arnold was appointed headmaster of Rugby, a school of no particular merit. He instituted a system of classical and general education with a strong emphasis on intellectual, moral, and religious discipline to prepare his students for the hazards of life. He also innovated the use of older students, as prefects, to govern the younger pupils. His methods, which were quite successful, were the model for other schools. Unfortunately, however, the very success of his methods delayed the establishment of a general educational system, a result which Arnold would not have wished.

In 1870 the **Forster Educational Act** was passed to provide for a general elementary education to all persons in England. Rather than a new system of education with separate buildings, this Act funded and improved existing church schools so long as the schools conformed to minimum standards. If no local school existed or the church school was inadequate, it provided means of establishing separate local schools. Within twenty years the number of schools doubled and could accommodate all those of school age. In 1891, attendance was made compulsory.

By the close of the nineteenth century, England had universal male suffrage, education available to all its citizens, and industrial production unsurpassed by any in the world. It was the head of a consortium of states, so that it was true that the sun never set on the British Empire.

18 THE HARVEST

The establishment of constitutionalism and an
unparalleled cooperation between all classes of
English bring to every citizen a wealth unknown
since the finest hours of the Roman empire.

The bedrock of the development of England and the English people is a marriage of the Germanic individuality and respect for others with the Celtic Hellenistic Christianity of self-worth and right of inquiry and expression. The "impassable barrier" of the surrounding oceans isolated England sufficiently for it to grow, but not so much as to prevent the arrival of new ideas conceived in other lands. Despite the invasions of Norsemen, be they Danes or Normans, the "hundreds" and the towns always retained some powers of home rule. Throughout all these years, and despite every obstacle so effectively employed on the continent, the English mind grew. Until the Renaissance, virtually all the efforts at enlightenment rested on an English base.

From its earliest years, and before Alfred, England offered a greater access to education to anyone. Measured by the Latin model, its schools were not so subordinated to a church as others in the sense that English schools were the least given to a fixed, rigid pattern of thought.

In the century from the death of Elizabeth to the accession of Anne in 1702, constitutionalism was established in England. James I had a corrupt and Italinate court. Charles I claimed a divine right of kingship based on the fiction of the Old Testament that God spoke to and selected kings. Such notions were inimical to both a private, practical people and to a parliament. On the heels of so radical a retrograde, that century saw the execution of a king, a civil war, a bloodless revolution, a short-lived republican government, and the return of the monarchy.

The result was the constitutional government which England and Great Britain have enjoyed to this day. In this interlude, the Puritans, using seeds grown in Dutch Protestantism, added stimulus to the notion of personal freedom. While the civil war of 1642-1648 was a religious war, the Reformation in England was largely political.

With the re-establishment of the monarchy, our quest is almost finished. We might think of it now as a loaf of bread. The ingredients have been mixed and kneaded. Now the mixture went into the oven to rise and bake.

Intellectualism came to full flower in this seventeenth century. the incorporation of Wales, Ireland and Scotland, with their preserved Celtic intelligence, were made a part of this mainstream. Secularization, democratization, and industrialization, marching hand-in-hand, under the aegis of British philosophic thought, brought England to the front ranks of the world of science. This was the age of Francis Bacon, Issac Newton, John Locke, Thomas Hobbes, and Adam Smith.

The English reaped enormously increased wealth. Per capita income far surpassed that of any other nation. Its historic interclass cooperation allowed access to anyone who was willing to work and take the risks of adventure. An exceptionally large number of the English people were in commerce, industry, or seafaring pursuits which encouraged their practical outlook without a rigid or doctrinaire overlord.

The Scotsman Adam Smith proved to be godsend as he was able to popularize the ideas of economic politics that the wealth of a society was its production rather than its treasury, that workers are also consumers, that while a person worked for one's own ends, society was the beneficiary, and that a free market place with its competition improved the condition of everyone. These notions were in stark contrast to the former commandment that a poverty-stricken group was a social necessity and wealth was counting coins. Overnight, it was acceptable for anyone to save, invest, and create new wealth.

The turbulence in the mother country from civil wars and unrest in the century before Anne sent the English to the four corners of the world which Elizabethan buccaneers such as Francis Drake, John Hawkins, and Walter Raleigh opened to them. A group need not be suppressed. It went to a colony, there to find wealth and grow under the protection of the crown to be partners to industry at home. Though the dictates of the Puritans might be strident and intolerant at home, away from English shores it was laissez faire, a natural outgrowth of the English way of a quiescent government with personal freedom, and a tolerant religion exercising few restraints on the mind.

The turbulence in England from a shifting and growing population bred by industrialization had to be solved by correcting the voting districts and correcting the voter lists. These changes were completed without the stains of civil bloodshed, as in France.

After the establishment of a constitutional monarchy, the English character came to its maturity. Two phenomena played a very important part in this development. First, Gildas, as we have seen, had written centuries earlier that "the island of Britain, situated on almost the utmost border of the earth, … is surrounded by the ocean, which forms… [an] impassable barrier, save on the south side, where the narrow sea affords a passage to Belgic Gaul." If we should pick up our globe again and notice England's position in relation to its neighbors, we can see that beyond London there is simply nowhere else to go in England, and nowhere to go through England. Dutens wrote in *Memoires d'un Voyageur* of the Countess de Boufflers' excursion to England early in the reign of George III: "It was to her credit that she was curious to see England, for it was noticed that she was the only French lady of quality who had made a trip there in the last two hundred years. None others in this class at all, neither the ambassadors' wives nor the Duchess of Mazarin had come except that it was necessary that they did." Many English persons outside London never saw a foreigner, while, in contrast, the character of Paris and Italy was much affected by tourists. Dutens also observed that "the manners of people of moderate fortune in England, are perhaps more comfortable to reason that those of any other nation that has come within my observation. They spend nothing upon ostentation; and if they have any luxury, it is that of convenience."

Combine this "isolation" at home with the growing wealth which enabled ever-increasing numbers to travel and seek the pleasures of life, and the English take on the character of persons who were reared as children of a secure, self-confident family: children who accept others but are enough of their own persons that their characters remain intact, possessing a sort of easy, self-assured, yet tolerant, carriage. Abroad, in unaccustomed climates and conditions, the dress of the English was the same as at home with only necessary accommodations to the heat or cold. Rarely did they learn a foreign tongue; rather, the colonials learned English. Often when they ventured to use a foreign tongue, it was to re-cast it in a familiar form. These people of so tiny number, who went abroad for even an extended colonial service, travelled as though on holiday, expecting an early return to the homeland, or they made a conscious effort to make the new abode as much like home as possible. Yet these things were done so that the natives could also participate in their English way of being. This steadfastness "to themselves" compensated for their small numbers and gave them such an enormous impact on the new territories.

The motto incised in stone at New College, Oxford, "Manners maketh man," sums up English qualities: a guarded reserve, a dislike of exaggerated amiability or courtesies, a reluctance to ask personal questions, and self-control. The English acquired "A fine aspect in fit array, / Neither too mean nor yet too gay." They had a genuine sense of tolerance unless one encroached into their private territory, but with a full knowledge of the absolute corollary: all the self-same notions of privacy of person must apply for the benefit of others. One cannot expect privacy and courtesy from another unless it be accorded to others.

Unlike their European cousins, who grew in a militarist feudalism under an interventionist spirit of a dominant religion, making a culture of conformism and obedience, the English "separateness of persons" was grounded in the ancient German personal code with the early notion of accountability even of a king, Hellenic self-worth, Pelagian self-reliance, blended with the old Celtic gentle manner and aggressive curiosity grown on an island fortress. This training ground fostered such thoughts as these from Richard Lovelace in "To Althea in Prison":

> Stone walls do not a prison make,
> Nor iron bars a cage…
> If I have freedom in my love,
> And in my soul am free,
> Angels alone, that sore above,
> Enjoy such liberty.

These qualities are England's legacy to America.

Index

S

Sarzana, Monk 43
Saxons 58, 62, 69, 77
Scholasticism 34, 45, 65, 99, 104
Scipio, Africanus 20
Scot, Michael 36
Settlement Act 122
Seven Years' War 128
Shakespeare, William 109
Sidon and Tyre 19, 20
Silvester II 36
Smith, Adam 121, 130, 134, 135, 146
Smith, John 119
Spanish Succession, War of 126, 128
Spenser, Edmund 110
Star Chamber 97, 106
Statute of Frauds 116
Stoicism 15, 16
Sumerians 4
Svegn 75

T

Tertullian 21, 65
Test Act 137
Thales 8
The War of the Roses 91, 95, 97
Thomas of Aquinas 45, 48, 88
Tiberius 13, 117
Toleration Act 121
Tyndale, William 110

U

Uccello, Paolo 48
Ulfilas 24
United States x, 128, 129

V

Valerian 23
Van Dyck, Anthony 50
Vasari, Giorgio 26
Venice 42
Victoria 140
Virgil 66

Virginia, State of 114, 119, 126, 127
Voltaire 37

W

War of the Roses 91, 95, 97
Washington, George 127
Watt, James 133
Wellesley, Richard 128
Wellington, Duke of 139
Whitby, Council of 66, 67, 77
Wilfred of York 77
William I 69, 73, 81, 97
William III 120, 125
William IV 137
William of Occam 88
Witan 59, 74, 82, 89
Wolsey, Thomas 99, 100, 101, 103
Women 25, 32, 58, 60, 111, 118
Wren, Christopher 117
Wycliffe, John 90

Y

York, Statutes of 27, 74, 75, 77, 89, 90, 95, 97, 134
York Monastery 64, 65, 66